THE LATIN ECLOGUES

GIOVANNI BOCCACCIO

The Latin Eclogues

Translated by David R. Slavitt

THE JOHNS HOPKINS UNIVERSITY PRESS
Baltimore

© 2010 The Johns Hopkins University Press
All rights reserved. Published 2010
Printed in the United States of America on acid-free paper
9 8 7 6 5 4 3 2 1

The Johns Hopkins University Press
2715 North Charles Street
Baltimore, Maryland 21218-4363
www.press.jhu.edu

Library of Congress Cataloging-in-Publication Data

Boccaccio, Giovanni, 1313–1375.
  [Buccolicum carmen. English]
  The Latin eclogues / Giovanni Boccaccio ; translated by David R.
Slavitt.
      p.   cm.
  ISBN-13: 978-0-8018-9562-3 (hardcover : alk. paper)
  ISBN-10: 0-8018-9562-6 (hardcover : alk. paper)
  ISBN-13: 978-0-8018-9563-0 (pbk. : alk. paper)
  ISBN-10: 0-8018-9563-4 (pbk. : alk. paper)
  1. Pastoral poetry, Latin (Medieval and modern)—Translations
into English.   2. Country life—Italy—Poetry.   3. Middle
Ages—Poetry.   I. Slavitt, David R., 1935–   II. Title.
  PQ4274.B7E5 2010
  872'.03—dc22   2009038865

A catalog record for this book is available from the British Library.

*Special discounts are available for bulk purchases of this book. For
more information, please contact Special Sales at 410-516-6936 or
specialsales@press.jhu.edu.*

The Johns Hopkins University Press uses environmentally friendly
book materials, including recycled text paper that is composed of at
least 30 percent post-consumer waste, whenever possible. All of our
book papers are acid-free, and our jackets and covers are printed on
paper with recycled content.

for Janet

CONTENTS

TRANSLATOR'S PREFACE

Most of what I have to say about these poems is in the translations—both in the way I have rendered Boccaccio's Latin and also in my italic intrusions where I am delivering information that may be helpful to readers. It may seem to be a weird way to proceed, but it puts Boccaccio and his friends and enemies of the trecento at a "pastoral" distance. When I did a version, many years ago, of Virgil's eclogues, I took liberties, mixed his poetry with my own commentary, and presented what were essentially a series of verse essays on the original poems. But they were Virgil's and were comparatively well known. Anyone who wanted the straight stuff could consult any number of available translations. These bucolic poems by Boccaccio, however, have not often been brought into English. I wanted to make it clear, therefore, what was his and what was mine. (Readers who choose to do so can keep me out of the way by confining their attention to the roman type.)

They are charming and engaging pieces, appealing as poems but also offering a wonderful insight into the life of Renaissance Italy. But whichever motive it is that prompts someone to look at these things, he or she is likely to be surprised and pleased by the other aspect. I have found delight in doing them, and it is the delight that, first and last, one wants to communicate.

I should probably say something about the different meaning that writing in Latin has had over the centuries. When Milton did it, or Marvell, or even John Owen the Elizabethan schoolmaster who was "the English Martial," it was a way of putting some parts of the audience at a distance, or a show-off gesture, or just perverse. Earlier, it was exactly the opposite, for a man of letters in Italy could not expect to be understood in Germany or Sweden, or Portugal, if he was writing in his own vernacular. But in Latin—which was then the Lingua Franca—there were no philological boundaries he had to negotiate (or be helped across by a translator). Dante, Petrarch, Boccaccio, and most of the writers of the time used one language or the other as they chose.

Where this leaves us in the twenty-first century, though, is that these elegant toys are accessible only to a very few Renaissance scholars and those fewer who are comfortable reading along in neo-Latin. These poems may not be great works, but they are fun, and Boccaccio is important and, maybe, even "great." So, while a reader may begin out of duty, he or she ought also to have a good time.

I have relied on Janet Levarie Smarr's translation (Garland Publishing, New York and London, 1987) and notes as a fine vade mecum. She is a better scholar than she is a poet, but I commend her book to those who want to learn more.

THE LATIN ECLOGUES

I ❧ Galla

DAMON:

Tindarus, what are you doing way up there near the Arno?
We here in Vesuvius' shadow or on the gentle
slopes of Monte Barbaro, watching our flocks and herds,
delight in our quiet lives. You were a sensible fellow.
How then could you leave what you knew well and loved
to try to better yourself on the flanks of the snowy alps?
Did your aspiration blind you to your contentment here?

TINDARUS:

I admit right away, dear friend, that one can be quite happy
in a humble hut or out in the woods living under the sky.
But the cruel sisters gave me a restlessness of mind
and I left to seek my fortune, leading Alcestus' bulls
to graze in his rich pastures. Here in the mezzogiorno
it's all too tempting to think that otherness is better.
But why do you look downcast? Why walk out alone
in the heat of the day when even lizards flee from the sun
to seek what shelter they can beneath the roadside brambles?

DAMON:

Don't ask. It's just too much. All I want now is to die.
Death is the foe of care and pain, and the last resort

for those who not only suffer but have no hope of relief.
Take care, my friend, and try to keep control of yourself.
Protect yourself from Cupid's quiver of poison arrows,
the slightest wound of which is enough to ruin a man.
All I ask from Fortuna is a quick and easy death.

TINDARUS:
Are you out of your tiny mind? Come let us sit down in this cave
where it's cool and I happen to have an agreeably bulging wineskin
with a good red.
              Phorba, go get us a couple of bowls.
You can see them up on the branch of the alder over there,
hanging by their handles as if they were succulent fruit.
    Meanwhile, Damon, tell me what grief weighs on your heart,
tormenting you. It often happens that telling the story
to someone who is able to share your pain can help,
for the burden is less if you do not have to bear it alone.

DAMON:
Maybe. I do remember Menalcas used to say so.
On the other hand, it seems clear that if I tell you the cause
of my pain then you will weep along with me. And the weight
of sadness will not be cut in half but rather doubled.

TINDARUS:
Don't trouble yourself with such gloomy thoughts. What are friends for?
Or ask what kind of person is only a friend to good fortune.

DAMON:
There was a nymph . . . Ah, Tindarus how can I tell you
how beautiful she was? Just as funereal cypress
yields to the green laurel, as tamarisk defers to
the pretty myrtle, so does Micon's famous statue
of Galathea give way to this young woman's perfection.

I remember the peaceful years when I rested among these beeches
without a care in the world, and with her happy band
of sister nymphs she found me, captivated, entranced,
and utterly subdued me. Those flashing eyes, those cheeks
with the delicate blush of a peach at its best moment . . . They kindled
a raging flame in my bosom from which I burn. Her touch
was like a blacksmith's bellows, making the fire grow hotter.
She brought me a quiver of arrows and a pack of dogs and implored me
not to go after dangerous bears or ferocious boars
with their sharp tusks but instead chase harmless little deer.
She made me exchange my hunting spears with their curved blades
for the bow that is so much safer and nets to trap the deer.
I didn't object at the time, but now, as I look back,
I think she went too far and that I should have refused her.
But then I wasn't thinking, was absolutely gaga,
and wanted only her many kisses and sweet embraces,
and I was content. Since then, she has turned away to tend
the flames in other hearts. She has abandoned me
and I die of shame and of love. I have my life again
but it's worthless now and joyless. Let the trees and hillsides
behold my death and bear witness to the great wrong she has done me,
and may the nymphs reprove her injustice and heartlessness.

TINDARUS:

No, no. You don't want to do such a thing. To commit
suicide for love? It never makes any sense,
as love doesn't make any sense either. But time will assuage
your pain. From the dead ashes, a flame can renew itself.
Your Adonis is cold now but he surely will burn again.

DAMON:

It isn't me; it's her. I'm afraid there can be no doubt
but that she threw me over for somebody else. I'm certain.
Deep in the woods on the lower slopes of Monte Ugo

there is a cave where Egon used to bring his flocks.
The goats were grazing or chewing their cud and he was playing
his reed flute. And I was out there on that day,
and I decided to leave my sheep in Phytia's hands,
as love, or let me be candid and admit it was jealousy really,
goaded me on. I'd heard the music of girls' laughter
and I'd seen that among them Galla was one of the playful girls
who were dancing their way toward that cave.
There was no reason at all for her to be heading that way,
or say there was no good reason. Meanwhile, Pamphylus, the goatherd,
led his flock to the grove of willows beneath the cliff
and in their shade sat down to play on his reed pipe
or now and then put that by to strum on his lyre instead.
He was, at least at first, playing for his own amusement,
and he's very good, I'm afraid. The music, however, changed
from random riffs to tunes and, as the poets would say,
the goats paused in their grazing to listen to him, and the kids
appeared to dance to his playing. To hell with the poets. He knew
that the girl was there and could hear him, and it was for her he performed,
certain that she was pleased and would come closer to hear
even more clearly. She did approach, and the wanton girl
sat down in the shade beside him. I'm watching this, remember,
and I can't believe my eyes. She thinks I'll never find out,
but there she is in broad daylight absolutely brazen,
with a couple of puppies romping about her and licking her hands.
I relaxed after a bit, as she called out to her companions,
and I told myself it was just the pretty spot and the music,
and it wasn't out of the question that she wanted them to enjoy it
along with her and share in her innocent delight.
But none of them came and she was still alone, adoring
his playing and him, as she gazed in the sweet shade of the trees
in what could have been admiration—or was it already longing?
She tossed her hair and ran her fingers through it. That trick

is what girls always use when they want men to notice their breasts'
attractiveness. (And we pretend we have no idea.)
She laughs that liquid laughter and gazes with deep brown eyes
in his direction. And then she reaches to touch his cheek
and she offers her face to be kissed, and the sound of the music stops.
She didn't know I was looking but couldn't be sure that I wasn't.
This is all out in the open, reckless with girlish abandon
or prompted by a desire she could not remember to hide.
O heavens! I'll say no more. And I wish I had seen no more,
and wish that Death might come to erase the dreadful image.

TINDARUS:
Your weeping will do you no good, as you know perfectly well.
Tityrus used to say that Love's thirst for the tears of men
could no more be satisfied than crickets out in the field
can be sated with dew. The sheep can never have too much clover.
The ability of the meadow to absorb the babbling brook's
water is endless. Take your cue from what you see
around you in nature. The leaves that autumn strips from the trees
the spring will give back. The wild south wind whips up the waves
that sooner or later Zephyr will calm again and the sea
that raged and swallowed ships will gleam in the bright sunshine
and dolphins will jump and play. This is how Fortuna
always works, by alternations, so that the wretched
she dashed down yesterday she may raise up tomorrow.
There will come a day, and I hope it may be soon,
when you will declare that no woodland shepherd could be
more fortunate than you. Believe me, and cease to weep.
Rely on the cures of time, and if they don't work there are others—
charms and potent herbs, or sometimes singing is helpful.
I have some of those old herbalists' recipes,
and I know a lot of tunes. And look, Phorba is coming
with that well-aged wine I spoke of. That can be useful too.

DAMON:

When sheep turn fierce and prey on the nearby goats, when wolves
raven upon hibiscus, when vultures swim in the sea,
and fish circle high in the air's updrafts, when farmers plow
their furrows in the sea, and sailing vessels turn
the earth in the spring for planting, then will the wanton girls
be steady in their affections and faithful to men who love them—
and only then will I want to call Galla back with herbs
or charms or pretty songs. I have been to Crete to climb
the highest Idalian peak, and ascended sacred Cithaeron
that looms over Boeotia, and I have gone to Paphos'
myrtle groves and, weeping, have hung my votive masks;
I've burned the incense and made the solemn vows to the gods;
and after all that I have sent my expensive gifts, but nothing
does any good at all. Nothing changes, and Love
only grows more cruel. And she grows crueler too.

TINDARUS:

Alas! It's a terrible business. Phorba brings us wine
and roasted chestnuts but look at this poor suffering fellow
whose head hangs low and whose very soul is beaten down.
In his heart that burned with love there are only ashes now.
I might as well be talking to the stones out here. But wait,
the pain will abate. There is life that will somehow spring up again.

DAMON:

Oh, Pamphylus, you son of a bitch! Why should it be you
to whom fickle Nature granted charms, talent, good looks,
and luck. You wave the pretty garlands of woodland flowers,
or sing and the animals listen, and the rivulets seem to hush.
I dare say you could make the mountain ash trees move
and rocks dance, and even the stolid mountains stir.
Why you? Even Love, who is cruel and likes to play nasty jokes,
defers to you or at least refuses to interfere

so that you can have your way with anyone you want.
Not even mighty Jove had such an easy passage
as you have come to expect almost as a matter of right.
Who but you could have lured the lovely Galla to join you
in Egon's cave? Who else could draw her into that grove
of delicate willow trees and all those secretive bushes?
O Great Father Silvanus, hear my fervent prayer:
let those yellow hairs she likes to comb and arrange
fade to white; let those smooth and delicate apple cheeks
wrinkle and lose their healthy glow! And soon, soon!
In the forest's darkest shadows may she find herself alone
and neglected so that I may come to her to mock
her trembling steps and her downcast eyes that are spilling tears.
Should you deny me this prayer, then grant me another and let me
be snatched by Death, who will take me where I may no longer feel
this burning pain. May shepherds bury my body and mark
my grave with a few lines of suitably mournful verse.

TINDARUS:
Love is a savage, too often the bane of innocent youth.
Look, he's collapsed. Bring water, somebody. Quickly!
I'll do whatever I can to revive him, the poor bastard.

II 🦢 Pampinea

MELAMPUS:
"What have I done wrong? What sin have I committed
to arouse your ire, Silvanus, god of the green woods?
Have I hacked at my staff with a biting hatchet for firewood?
Have I chased bears across your meadows to foul the springs
or frighten the playful nymphs so that I should suffer your wrath?
The groves and fields are hushed now, the crickets subside and hide
in the vineyard; in this heat the birds have fallen silent;
the plowman takes the yoke from the necks of his weary oxen
and leads them into the shade to wait for the midday swelter
to abate at least a little. Only I am driven,
unable to pause in my relentless and stupid quest,
a wretched plaything of Love, as I search for Pampinea,
trying to follow her footprints, or, first, trying to find them.
It's a quest, but so far totally unsuccessful. I cannot
worry about my meager savings. I cannot think
of anything else as I wander the highest mountain passes
or hack my way through the underbrush of pathless forests.
I haven't the vaguest idea what is in front, but passion
hounds from behind and keeps me faring forever forward
looking for any clue, any plausible place she might be,
or anyone who has seen or heard of her having passed by.
Now and then I can look down into a valley and see

a group of hunters or, rather, the distant dust cloud their passage
has raised into the air. Sometimes I startle the goats
that cavort on the rocks above me, or long-eared hares in the scrub.
I come across nets that someone has spread to catch the deer,
and servants, or packs of dogs, but no one I ask has seen her.
I stop and shield my eyes as I peer into the distance,
and I call, 'Pampinea!' and wait, and call, 'Pampinea!' again.
But nothing, not even an echo. The sound travels up to the heavens
from which there is no reply—as if the gods too were deaf.
One might suppose that her name gets caught now and then in the
        branches
of trees and fills the valley. I know I deceive myself,
but there have been times when the wind made a soft noise in those trees
that I could not help but suppose was the sound of her approach,
but I am deceived once more and as deeply disappointed
as I was all those other times. It's Love who plays those tricks
on gullible people like me who labor in her service.
   "How can this happen? O you forest nymphs, explain
why nature is kind to the beasts of the field and the birds in the air
but plays these games that try the patience and souls of men?
We see how the animals mate with an enviable ease,
the ram going after the ewe and the bull seeking out his darling
heifer. Or we look up to see how the turtledove
follows his heart's delight into the towering branches
where both of them coo together in harmonious concord.
But the shepherd has no such luck. Only to him is pleasure
offered but then denied in that torture Tantalus knows,
ensnared by the smiles and even the kisses of pretty girls
who then ignore and shun him, or mocked with derisive laughter.
   "Ah, satyrs and fauns, who have been my longtime friends and
        companions,
what advice can you give me? What comfort can you offer?
How can I find any cheer in the simple lives of my sheep?
What solace is there for me in pleasant woodlands or valleys?

Those cool caves in which I sometimes used to take shelter
in the heat of the day mean nothing now. My body is all
out of kilter so that I shiver with chills at noon
or burn as I would with a fever in the cool of a spring evening.
I yearn for her and I feel great fear lest she come to harm.
Has she tripped on a rock? Has some wild beast emerged from the forest
to attack her pretty body? Has somebody bolder than I am
dragged her off by force or persuaded her with kisses
that cloud her mind? We know how mischievous Cupid can be.
The silence of country scenes can be nothing more than illusion,
for drama and sometimes violence can happen here, and they do,
as some nymph comes passing through a secluded dell with her skirts
tucked up to show her knees, her hair streaming out in the wind
with its garlands of myrtle askew . . . Who would not then be seized
by the sudden fires that Venus can kindle in any man's heart?
That she is alone out there and the afternoon light is fading
only serves to encourage whatever the casual suitor
may find himself imagining and asking himself, why not?
The beautiful Aegla, the daughter of the king of the Lapiths, Apollo
loved was no more attractive than my sweet Pampinea.
The exquisite Neaera, that nymph by whom Apollo begot
Phaethusa and Lampetie was lesser in beauty than she.
Her complexion is somewhat dusky, but the forest sets that off
or rather it serves to show what Nature herself prefers.
Those lovelies I have mentioned captured the notice of Jove
or Apollo as well as Argus. But the gods these days descend
less often than was their wont in ancient times. Instead,
I worry about the men she is likely now to encounter,
Corydon or maybe the ruddy-cheeked Alexis
would surely find her attractive, want her, and offer her gifts—
nothing vulgar of course, but tokens of their affection
of the kind that women like, and goddesses too, and they look
in a kindly way at the man whose thoughtfulness is so touching.
    "What can I do? I am helpless. Life everywhere is risky.

As the wolves are the curse of the stables, and hail comes down on the
   orchards,
and the northern wind blows hard to upset the pregnant goats,
my bane is Love, which is also cruel and delights to drive me,
burning, tormented, distracted, contorted, and swept away.
And how to escape? I haven't the least clue! My heart
wishes only for peace. I want to be left alone
to let my mind and body recover their strength and balance.
I heard the ominous crow that brought bad news to Minerva
warning me from a branch of an oak but I dismissed it.
What does a bird know? How can he tell me my future?
I'm less skeptical now and more than sufficiently chastened.
   "My love, my darling, my dearest jewel, where do you roam
among these craggy mountains? What wild animals' lairs
tempt you with your bow and quiver of accurate arrows?
What keeps you so far away? Do you rest, perhaps, in the shade
in some faraway forest? Had Fortune been kinder to me,
she might have allowed me to go along with you on the hunt.
I'm good at setting nets for the deer, and I'm also good
driving the spear deep into the boar. I know
how to kill the stag that the arrows have wearied and pull its antlers
back to dispatch it quickly. I can manage the dogs or drive
wild goats into the nets. Nasilus taught me his tricks
in woods that are far distant and prepared me well for this work.
Could not Diana grant me that I might be one of your party,
even the least of your servants? When you take your midday rest
I could sprinkle water to settle the dust on the ground
or strew the floor of the cave with soft reeds from the marshes.
Or, if you'd rather bid me prepare you a *dejeuner*
sur l'herbe, I could set forth the baskets of ripe fruit,
the jugs of milk, the wineskins, and bread of course in baskets.
And afterward a nap? Certainly, dear lady.
I'd gather branches of willow or tamarisk, or myrtle
for a soft and fragrant couch upon which you might lie down.

And flowers! Oh, flowers, of course! Violets, bright narcissus,
strewn about or else in nosegays for you to carry.
And as you lie there waiting for sweet sleep to attend you,
I'd hush the barking dogs, brush all the gnats away,
and whisper pleasant stories to occupy your mind.
Would Corydon do all this? Or Alexis? Or would Glaucus,
at whom I have seen you looking and taking rather more notice
than I might like? Oh, tell me, my darling Pampinea,
why do you steal away with your irresistible face
upon which I wish to plant the sweetest kisses? Why
flee from one who adores you? Why frustrate such a love?
   "I inquire of local shepherds and ask what nymphs I encounter
whether they have perhaps seen you. Which way were you going?
In what direction? And then, with a heavy heart, I inquire
with whom you might have been walking. Opheltes laughed at me
and said that, 'You look in the woods and up on the mountain foothills,
but Pampinea and Glaucus have gone off together to find
themselves some cozy cave. Palemon, you are pathetic.'
Oh, God! I felt as though I'd been struck by a hard blow
and I had no choice but to give myself up to pain and gasp
in agony. I lay on the ground and my body writhed
helplessly, for I had been overcome and undone.
   "Diana, if you remember the special delight you took
coming down every night to see Endymion's beauty,
if we have honored your altars and hung in the beech tree branches
the supple bows you like, turn your wrath upon me
and do me the great kindness of ending my pain with death.
Finish me off with your arrows that never err. No more
those sweet songs with the pipes, the satisfactions of labor,
or the chase and its excitement. I started the hare from the briars,
but lazy Glaucus has caught it and he has bagged my prey.
Empty-handed I pour out tears on these rough rocks
that fell from the weathered cliffs. I wail my bitter laments
the indifferent wind snatches and scatters in empty space.

"You ancient oaks, and you the long-standing ilex,
all you trees of the forest, you connoisseurs of sighing,
hear the bitter complaint of Palemon, and grant to him
death's anodyne. The gods of the skies and nymphs of the wood
have turned deaf ears to my prayers, and the simple woodland spirits
have likewise turned away, indifferent or pitiless. I
kneel down before you, therefore, and hope that your hard bark hides
softer hearts that might show mercy to one who suffers.
If one of you may be weary of thirsting for rain, of axes
that lop your branches, or goats that nibble your delicate leaves,
and you share my distaste for any further earthly involvement,
fall upon me and crush me, and let us go out together.
Only my death can untangle this knot of hurt in my heart.
O Death, you cruel, recalcitrant, arbitrary being,
why won't you come when called? Only you can relieve
this madness of mine. Young as I am, I cannot bear it
and wish it to end. I invite you, but you disdain to come.
And you, Pampinea, who used to carve in the beech tree bark
our intertwined initials to commemorate our embraces,
you who complained and lamented when I was forced to depart
and clung to me with the added passion of sweet regret,
accept from me this final gift, which is my wish
that you enjoy your youth before it decays. New flowers
come to the meadow in spring, and green grass grows again,
but the sad truth remains that time only runs one way,
as Lycoris used to observe, back before he had aged
to the foolish, white-haired creature he's now become, a ghost
already except that he still breathes and glares in rage.
None of that for me. I'm happy to die—as I think
you want me to do. No longer would I be a nuisance but only
a kind of a ghastly trophy. I'll spare myself old age
and Thestylis will weep and adorn my funeral bust
with garlands of woodland flowers. Perhaps you, too, will spare
a blossom or two, and perhaps some witty epitaph

for the sorry life of a man who loved you and tried to please.
But until Death comes to take me, I cannot help myself:
I shall follow you wherever you go in the mountains and woods
and dewy fields. I shall not be far away but shall dwell
in those empty mountains and woods, those forlorn dewy fields."

    These are the words that Palemon, undone by his great grief,
poured out with many tears by the shady banks of the Arno,
watching the implacable water flow on to Pisa.
But evening was coming on. It was now time for me
to drive the goats and their frolicking kids back to their pens.

III 🎵 Faunus

PALEMON:

Pamphylus, you're taking your ease, snug in the cave of your fathers
even though the entire forest trembles, hearing the angry
shouts of Testilis. Are you not worried at all, yourself?

Palemon is perhaps Boccaccio, or an aspect
along with his friend Pamphylus of that authorial voice.
The eponymous Faunus, meanwhile, is Forlì's Ghibelline ruler,
Francesco degli Ordelafi. In 1347
he left to join with Ludwig, the King of Hungary, who
was on his way to invade Naples. His brother, Prince Andrew,
who as you will no doubt recall, was married to Joan
(to whom the throne had devolved from her grandfather Robert the Wise),
but she didn't care for Andrew and was said to have been unfaithful.
Ludwig was most displeased and wanted his brother to rule,
although a great many Italians proved to be loyal to Joan—
although not Francesco of Forlì. He's probably called "Faunus"
because he was fond of hunting. You've got all that? Okay?
Oh, I'm afraid that there's one more name that will come up:
"Testilis," which has a nice Vergilian ring.
She is Forlì personified, troubled by Faunus' departure
and criticizing the ruler for gallivanting around.

PAMPHYLUS:

What are you, drunk? Your battered tankard has lost its handle
and you have lost your wits. Worry about your pigs
that are likely even now to be ruining grain in the fields.
Never mind the rumors that are spreading throughout the woods.
You have, I think, more pressing, if rather more modest concerns.

PALEMON:

I admit to dozing off every now and again, but I wasn't—
I am not—drunk. But it makes no difference what you think,
having just reawakened yourself. Listen to me.
(I assume that your mistress Licisca will not object.)

PAMPHYLUS:

Sit down, sit down. Let's let the insults go. Tell me
what is it that you have heard? What is this bad news?

PALEMON:

I was out in the woods doing the usual woodland things
in the standard pastoral setting, watching the nanny goats nurse
their playful kids. I was making acanthus garlands and also
verses I thought might entertain Mopsus, my dear friend.

*For Mopsus, we can read Petrarch, and the acanthus leaves he's picking
are evergreen but not quite the laurel Petrarch wears.*

And into this paradigmatic rural setting there comes
Testilis, clearly upset and complaining to all who could hear her:
"Oh, Faunus, Faunus! What madness has overthrown your mind
that you should go chasing bears through the rugged forests? Remember
your little children who laugh and play in the pleasant meadows!
It troubles a mother's heart to think of their helplessness.
Do you not worry at all for their safety when you are gone?

Think of the Allobrogian wolves howling in fury.
How can I hope to fight them off, a woman, defenseless,
with only a few Molossian hounds for my protection?"

Allobrogian wolves? Yes, the Allobrogi
lived in Gaul, so these are agents of Avignon,
possibly the papal legates at work down in Romagna.

PAMPHYLUS:
Are you at all surprised? What else could she have expected?
Faunus has always been fond of adventure. In love with danger,
he has always braved the darkest woods and most dangerous monsters.
Would Testilis' complaints have been likely to hold him back?

PALEMON:
That's what I came here for, to hear your views and discuss
what we may now expect. But look, Moeris is coming,
leaning on his staff as he shuffles along toward us.

Moeris, no doubt deserves a gloss. His figure stands
more or less for Checco da Mileto de' Rossi, Boccaccio's
friend and also Francesco's trusted secretary.

Greetings, Moeris. Join us. You come at an opportune time.
Sit for a while and tell us what is the latest gossip.
Do you happen to know, for instance, why Testilis is angry?

MOERIS:
That's not what I'd call news. Testilis and Faunus
are quarreling all the time at the top of their voices. The leaves
of the oak trees near their windows shrivel and fall at their din.
You're asking if birds sing or if billy goats ever chew.

PAMPHYLUS:

Yes, yes, I know. They are figures of fun, and I have laughed
often enough at their expense. But sit and rest.
Set down your staff. Come out of the heat of the merciless sun.
At this time of day the mountains provide no shadow. The lizards
hide wherever they can in the shade of the rocks. But here
in the cave there's a cool spring, and you can refresh yourself.
The tradition around these parts, as you certainly know yourself,
is that Amintas once rested in this very cave.
Let us sing sweet songs together and play on our pipes.

Amintas, we may suppose, is none other than Dante.

MOERIS:

Me? Sing in these woods? It's a bad time, I'm afraid,
and the only songs are the crickets' chirr and the crows' caws.

PAMPHYLUS:

So what? Let the swineherds wallow in gloom and doom. For us
the world is whatever our songs can make it. For Mopsus' sake,
for the Muses' sake, and the stars', let us not be deterred
and let us maintain our faith that what we do is important.

PALEMON:

I wish I could. I'm afraid my duties require attention.
In heat like this, I must bathe my flock in the nearby stream,
which isn't the kind of thing that's conducive to pleasing the Muses.
Cidypes is obsessive and counts the kids every day.

MOERIS:

I have a Cidypes too, who's always giving instructions
to lead the lambs to a certain spring, or to feed them on clover,
or else to take willow branches to feed the cows in his herd.
But I say to hell with him. Pines will grow out of the sea,

tigers will file in peace into their pens, and lions
will flee from the fierce deer and wolves from the menacing goats
before I allow my work to get in the way of my art.
But that's for another time. Let us discuss the tumult
that's everywhere in the forest. Sit for a while, and listen.
   You know that wooded plain down in the mezzogiorno
between the two seas. Argus used to live there.

Argus is Roberto il Saggio, Joan's grandfather,
the late King of Naples (obit 1343).

An admirable shepherd, he had a thousand flocks
and no one knew better than he how to predict the weather,
or which leaves were good for the sheep and which were unhealthy.
He was a splendid singer with a sweet voice but also
skilled at the pipes and strings, so good that Apollo himself
might on Mount Olympus worry about competing
with such a gifted musician. The cruel Fates snatched him away
and took him up to the stars as his virtues richly deserved.

We're supposed to think of Macrobius, who says in some commentary
that the souls of virtuous men ascend to the stars after death.

The mountains wept for him and the fauns and satyrs mourned.
Apollo himself regretted the loss of such a man.
Argus bequeathed his woods and fields to young Alexis.

Well, no, he didn't. Boccaccio has got this detail wrong.
"Alexis" stands for Andrew, the husband of Queen Joan.
It was Joan to whom he left the throne. Andrew just sat
beside her, and maybe walked a couple of steps behind her
as we've seen Prince Philip doing. It isn't a difficult job,
but maybe with Andrew's machismo, it began to get annoying.

Alexis went into the forest on a dark and stormy night
and a pregnant wolf sprang out from the brush and clamped her jaws
around his neck. It hung on until the poor fellow was dead.

The baroque hasn't started yet, but this is bizarre enough:
Joan is the pregnant wolf. She had been knocked up,
not by her husband, but probably Louis of Taranto.
Andrew, who day by day was more of a pain in the neck
(to follow Moeris' figure) was strangled and flung from a window,
the idea being to make it look like an accident,
but everyone at the court assumed that Joan was to blame.
After all, a natural death? Think of the odds
against that kind of thing in the trecento in Naples.

Or else it could have been lions or one of those great wild boars
that roam in those parts of the forest.

                              Lions and boars are barons,
worried that Andrew could somehow seize the throne and its power.

If I told you every detail of what those shepherds and goatherds
were doing down there, I'm afraid I should have to keep on going
all afternoon and night and I still wouldn't finish by morning.
When, in the hollow cliffs along the Danube, Tityrus
heard about the death of his son he was deeply grieved.

Tityrus, of course, is Ludwig, who isn't an interloper
but brother to Andrew, or, keeping the pastoral names, Alexis.
They're related to Roberto and are all from the house of Anjou.

Tityrus gnashed his teeth and summoned his toughest plowmen
and fiercest dogs to attack this unruly part of the woods
to put down the prowling wolves and get rid of the tawny lions.

You must remember seeing them pass by on their way
with their gleaming hunting spears and their nets upon their shoulders.

PALEMON:
You mean the men of Hyster and those from Chalcidia too?

This is pastoral/florid for men who come from the Danube
and those who come from Cumae, or actually Naples.

What damage did they do on the banks of the Eridanus?

And that, of course, is the poor monosyllabic Po.

MOERIS:
Many men from around these parts follow Tityrus
with hunting dogs and spears—Faunus, for instance, for whom
Testilis wails in vain as she summons him home with shouts
that resound throughout the woods. Nevertheless, he's going
with hardly a thought to his people's wishes and even their safety.
You can still see the dust cloud that hangs in the motionless air
where he and his men have passed not very long ago.

PAMPHYLUS:
Lunatics are often impulsive like that. I'm afraid
that, crazy or not, Faunus is a man who cannot sit still.
What will come of all this? I cannot imagine good.
Testilis will grow old and increasingly feeble, I fear,
but who can say? I hope more fortunate stars may shine.

PALEMON:
Who can control hot-blooded youth or teach them wisdom?
Old men rest in the square and mothers sit in their doorways,
but Anaritius says somewhere that the high praise men

desire is that which is won abroad. You're staying here,
but I'm going after Faunus to do whatever I can.
Look after my flocks, if you would, and keep an eye on my holdings.

PAMPHYLUS:
Of course. I'm happy to help, as a friend should do for a friend.
Good luck, and come home soon and safe. Take care of yourself.

It's messy. It can't contain the intrigue, greed, and violence
the pastoral mode was never meant to accommodate.
Faunus' support of Tityrus was more a matter of lucre—
he resented having to pay the tribute the Church and the Guelfs
demanded, and Ludwig, succeeding, could have put a stop to all that.
Ludwig came in and did all right. Joan fled to Provence,
where she was later murdered. Ludwig cut off some heads.
Francesco, meanwhile, had to hurry home to Forlì,
which was under attack, as even the simple shepherds expected.
In the end, he fell off his horse and he died a few days later.
A catastrophe all around, from which our soi-disant shepherds
couldn't derive any simple pastoral truths. Never mind.
It isn't only the eclogue but poetry itself
that cannot make any sense of the world when the dominant figure
turns out to be Yersinia pestis, *from Jaffa, which spread*
throughout Europe in 1348 to bring
the Black Death, the first great plague—that horror from which
the seven men and the three women fled from Florence
to the country villa's safety, to tell one another the stories
Boccaccio reports in his Decameron.

IV 🐚 Dorus

MONTANUS:

Slow down there, Dorus! What are you chasing? Or running away from?
Have you lost a goat or a cow? Five minutes one way or another
won't make much of a difference. Rest. At least catch your breath.
There's time. The evening star has not yet shown itself.

DORUS:

Give me a break, Montanus. I'm running as fast as I can,
pressed by my terror of who or what could be chasing me.

MONTANUS:

Out here in this remote and idyllic place? You're joking.
Or else you're carrying money, which makes everyone nervous.
Even so, my cave is safe with its mouth shielded
by privets. Unless someone knows it's there, he's likely to miss it.
There's a cook-fire going inside and amphorae of well-aged wine.
There's grain, and cheese, and a lot of goat milk. Come in and rest.
You're out of breath, after all. And here is your chance to recover.

DORUS:

I appreciate the offer, but if I may say so, you sound
just a bit smug. You think your pastoral life out here
is calm and secure, but you have no idea what Fortune

has in mind for you in a year or in ten minutes.
Nothing that we rely on is trustworthy or safe,
for danger is everywhere and there's no place a man can hide.

PHYTIAS:
If that's all you want, then why do you not accept his offer?
At this height, we can look out on a prospect of Pisan fields
and Tuscan flocks and herds. To the north we can see the Alps.
On a clear day we can make out the Ligurian hills and can trace
the course of the Rhone along which those red-capped people dwell . . .

The red-capped people are not meant to be exotic
Auslanders (like Finns that Tacitus speaks of, who keep
their children in nests high in the trees and out of danger).
Boccaccio, less far-fetched, is talking of Avignon,
where the cardinals are assembled. Dorus, the man who is fleeing,
is Louis of Taranto, a claimant to Naples' throne.
Montanus, who lives on the mountain, is anyone from Volterra,
where Louis sought refuge. And "Phytias" is not, after all, a typo,
but Boccaccio's rendition of Pythias, Damon's friend.
The name is a label for Niccola Acciaiuoli, Louis'
grand seneschal who never abandoned his king and friend.
"Dorus," he thought, meant "bitter," but there I'm afraid he was wrong.

DORUS:
My hope had been to go on till I reached the peaceful Arno,
of the beauty of which you have often spoken with special fervor,
and I thought to seek sanctuary from the fortunate Florentines.

PHYTIAS:
I did, indeed, but now, having seen how the deer have turned
wolfish, I am cautious and, frankly, even afraid.
Everywhere I turn I see there are perils lurking.

How do you get an eclogue to include the information
that Acciaiuoli's cousin happened to be the Bishop
of Florence, and he had hoped that his family connections
might persuade the Florentines to help his king—
but no, they were all afraid of Ludwig and wouldn't allow him
to enter and thus endanger the peace that Dorus craved.

MONTANUS:
But come into my cave. You can rest and recount your troubles.
I may not be able to do much more than listen, but still
a burden that's shared can seem a little bit lighter sometimes.
Galathea will fix us something to eat. Okay?

DORUS:
It's beyond all imagination, how Fortune has worn me down.
Think of savage tigers prowling your pleasant pastures
to maul the pregnant ewes or even the strongest bulls,
or picture a sudden plague sent down by a vengeful heaven
that wipes out all your chickens and leaves them dead in the coop
giving off such a stench that you cannot bear to approach them.
What I have gone through is worse, and I further torture myself
by thinking of all I have lost and cannot hope to regain.
An exile, impoverished, I now wander the hostile earth
relying on friends who betray me as often as not, or strangers
like you who on some occasions are courteous and kind.
I am either on the verge of weeping, or else, and worse,
of spewing forth the foulest curses that I can think up.

MONTANUS:
Be brave, my man—which is easy to say and hard to do—
but even the worst hardships cannot overthrow a great
and steady mind that ought to control the tender heart.

DORUS:

Think of what Argus possessed: the rich fields of Campania,
and those that the Volscians tilled, the olive groves of Lucania,
the Samnite pastures, the rugged Brutian hills and cliffs,
and all of that rough land the poor Calabrians scratch at,
the fields that belonged to Daunus and Pelignus' pleasant streams . . .

Argus is still King Robert, and his holdings are here described
in literary garb, using the ancient names,
with the Volscians being the Romans to whom Aeneas came.
The rest of the places are down in the south, but the main idea
is that Robert had a great deal of territory and power.

Prince of all that was Argus, a shepherd with many flocks
and grazing lands that extended as far as the eye could see.
He could also play the pipes so the tallest trees would bend
to catch the faintest notes. A paragon among men,
he died, or say that he left us to hide himself in heaven.

This is a stretch, for Robert wasn't himself a writer,
although he did an essay on the poverty of Christ
and all the apostles. A patron of writers and scholars, the king
deserves at least at secondhand Boccaccio's praise.

Soon after he died the poor Alexis followed
and Phytias here arranged a marriage between myself
and the fair Liquoris, so that Argus' grandchildren retained
his ancient fields as well as his thriving flocks and herds.

Alexis is still Prince Andrew, the one who got strangled and thrown
out of a window or possibly down some long stone staircase.
Liquoris is Queen Joan, Andrew's wife and then widow,
not any model of virtue but neither was she a drunk

as the curious name suggest. What it means in Greek is "twilight,"
and this is only Boccaccio's strange version of Virgil's
Lycoris, who appears in Gallus (Eclogue X).

No pastures anywhere were better or richer than those
of the great Argus, but Erinys set us all to brawling
and Polyphemus from far away on the banks of the Hyster,
raised, it is said, on the milk of savage beasts, attacked us.

You getting all this? It needs a gloss perhaps? You know
that Erinys is a fury, or sometimes the name can mean
all three of them together. And Polyphemus? That's Ludwig,
who earlier was Tityrus but now the code has changed.
(Dante uses the name for Bologna's Guelph ruler.)
The Hyster is still the Danube. That Ludwig was nursed on the milk
of wild beasts is only the usual way to suggest
that he has a primitive strength and isn't like you or me.

Falling upon the peaceful meadows, he is a torrent
of righteous rage as his anger pours down like swollen streams
in springtime when the swirling waters ignore their banks
and run on a rampage hurling rocks and even boulders,
uprooting trees, and spreading terror wherever they go.
He was like that and punished the guilty but did not stop there,
for after he'd fouled their protesting faces with bloody gashes,
he turned to the innocent, killing such good men as Paphus,
or he gathered the lads who had spent their days pursuing nymphs
and heaped his chains upon them and shipped them home as captives.

Paphus is Charles of Durazzo, the Duke of Calabria. Ludwig
had him beheaded if only because he was a relation,
a cousin, and therefore a possible threat. The others, the "lads,"
were Neapolitan princes, the brothers of Louis and Charles.

It seems to us rather brusque, but this is the Turkish system,
which one could defend for saving, in the long run, many lives
that otherwise would surely have been lost in civil wars.

Think of one of those monsters in children's stories with huge
teeth and terrible claws, some flying dragon. He rips
the fruit from the trees in the orchards and breaks their boughs with his
     teeth;
he frightens the birds from the skies with his loud shrieks, and he opens
gates and locks to get at the flocks; he fleeces the sheep
and then disembowels the ewes, while he swallows their lambs whole.
If he does not kill the bulls, he removes their dangerous horns.
Ceres' sacred oaks and the caverns Lyceus loves
he loots and then destroys in his hot and reckless fury.

Ceres is maybe Mary, and Lyceus is a name
for Apollo, which we can translate into a corresponding
Christian figure, so that he could be Jesus. The point
is that the oaks and the caverns are surely churches, or even
specific churches that Ludwig's soldiers raided or razed.

Into the woods, he drove the satyrs, the nymphs, and the fauns
that used to romp in the verdure. The Fates or the ominous stars
are possible explanations. Or there may be none at all.

MONTANUS:
Alas! I remember a song that the plowboys used to sing
about how quarrels can bring us all down together.

PHYTIAS:
Where is that mastering mind you were talking about before?

MONTANUS:
You may have it, my friend, but freely I confess
that I am flesh and blood, and my mind does not always order
what my heart may feel. Only this afternoon,
while Lycas was cutting brushwood with his long pruning hook,
Coridon was speaking of these distressing events
to Amintas, who was watching the flocks out in the meadow.
I wasn't even certain that any of it was true,
but it was bad enough news so that the tears welled up
in these old eyes. Now that all they said is confirmed,
how can I maintain that stiff upper lip the Stoics
so much admire. Let me feel what I feel as Dorus
tells me all the details, to which I shall listen in anguish.

*These are just random names from Virgil that stand for friends
and neighbors there in Volterra. Pay them no special mind.*

DORUS:
The woodlands' beauties are being wrecked and the shepherds and flocks
are fleeing hither and thither and sometimes yon, trying
to save themselves from the rapidly spreading catastrophe.
Fear is everywhere and no one knows what to do.
Some head for the hills while others go deep in the woods
to hide in caves they may know of. Some, in desperation,
join with the monster's forces and pledge their faith to him,
hoping to find some measure of mercy for those they love.
Yet others rely on the gods—if there are any gods, that is—
to give him their just chastisement for what he has done and is doing.
Nays, who is pregnant, flees with her twins and barely escapes
the wicked man's cruel hands as she hurries all through the night
seeking shelter from friends or strangers and pale with fear.
Ah, Montanus, you weep, as Phytias warned you not to.
Involuntary tears stream down your face. How can I
go on with this? It pains me even more than you.

Nays is Queen Joan's sister Maria. She is a widow
now that Charles of Durazzo's head has been lopped off.
She did indeed flee to the monks at Santa Croce.
From there disguising herself in the habit of one of the monks
she went on to France, which was safe and where she was able to wait
for Naples' weather to change. This melodramatic stuff
can't be easily managed in eclogues, which is a shame.
It isn't every night that you meet a pregnant monk.

MONTANUS:

I'm not at all surprised. I understand your distress.
But, still, try to go on. It may, in the end, be helpful.

PHYTIAS:

I concur altogether with the young man's suggestion. Tell us
what else has happened. Surely, you have no flocks to tend,
and we're safe with him. Let us rest for a while as you speak further.

MONTANUS:

What I most want to hear, or most dread hearing, is how
your friends conducted themselves. Were Paphus' claims of valor
merely boasts and bluster? Did he give proof of his courage,
fighting against the monster with his great spear? Or Asylas?
Or Phorbas, the good shepherd? Or Damon, our old friend?
What about you, for that matter, or Phytias? Did you fight
as well as you all could? I cannot doubt that Pamphylus
and Molorcus and so many others were close at your side. I've seen them
at boxing and wrestling matches, and races, shouting and cheering!
Or now that these competitions have turned suddenly real,
did all of them scuttle away to try to save themselves?

DORUS:

What can I say? They failed me, every one of them. Only
Phytias here remained steadfast and loyal. He still

is with me as you see, following me in my flight.
He was prepared to attack and I had taken an arrow
from the quiver I carry, had fitted it onto the bowstring, and drawn
the heavy bow when he looked about and realized
that no one else had come to our call of alarm. Not one!
He stopped me, saying that I could bend the wood of the bow
but not the will of the Fates. What Jupiter has foreseen
we cannot try to avoid or change. We had to flee.
I listened to him and saw that he was right. We left
our homes, our forests, our flocks to the ravages of that monster
and sailed in a fragile boat to be tossed by the winds and the waves
until we reached Talamone, a port close to Siena.
From there we have made our cautious way to arrive at your fields.

From Siena they went to the Acciaiuoli holdings near Florence,
but the Florentines were worried and refused them permission to enter,
let alone stay for a while, and they had to continue their journey
to Avignon, where they lived as guests of Clement VI.

MONTANUS:
It grieves me to hear this, and I welcome you here for as long
as you find it convenient to stay. At the top of that tall oak tree
a crow announces the truth, which is that you will return
and recoup. Your prospects are bleak just now. But do not despair.
Before the Delphic laurel sits once again on your brow,
you must offer the shades a human head you have cut
with a farmer's well-honed sickle. But we will say no more.
Let us turn to rites of Bacchus now and drink
the good wine that I spoke of. Galathea is calling.
The ewes and the little lambs are ambling back to their fold,
and the sky, which was a cerulean blue, is fading to black.

What head should he cut with a sickle? Nobody seems to know.
Montanus' interpretation, sanguine and sanguinary,

is misleading. Ludwig leaves Naples, and Louis and Joan return;
Ludwig returns, and Louis and Joan then have to leave;
then Ludwig goes home, and Louis and Joan of course come back.
They are crowned again in Naples. Louis goes off to subdue
Sicily, but barons back on the mainland revolt.
Louis comes home and defeats them, but then, at this point, dies.

V 🦢 The Falling Forest

CALIOPUS:
Look at you there, Pamphylus, lolling that way on the greensward
and thinking no doubt of love—Chalcidia's, I daresay,
but I should be altogether surprised if, in her thoughts,
you figured at all. She's mourning, instead, for her poor lost forest.

PAMPHYLUS:
What are you talking about? Here, sit down by me.
Phoebus' horses have mounted high, and the goats need shade.

CALIOPUS:
Not long ago in Sicily, as I wandered through the woods
and the flowering countryside, I thought I heard the sound
of a woman weeping, and, yes, it proved to be so. I searched
until I could find the source of this bitter lamenting, and soon
confronted her, Chalcidia, stretched out on bare ground,
choked with tears and groaning at every exhalation.
Think of a lovely blossom drooping in noon heat,
or, without any tropes or figures, think of a girl, distraught.

PAMPHYLUS:
Alas, I know how she feels. I share her dismay at how
the pines have been blasted by lightning and burnt in the forest fires.

Dogs that guard the sheep have turned on them and killed them.
All night long we hear the howling of hungry wolves.
The times are bad. I wonder what is the point of living.
But tell me, what did she say? What can you remember?
I should be most grateful for whatever you can recall.

CALIOPUS:
I am happy to tell you. Faithful Amintas here can watch
the flocks a while and make sure that the goats don't get into mischief.
If Bavius gets riled, he'll sic Corilas on them
to bite the kids and terrify the helpless lambs.

PAMPHYLUS:
Amintas has a stick or can throw stones at the dog.

CALIOPUS:
She called on the fauns and her sister nymphs but there was no
reply, not even the echo of her own forlorn appeals.
She beat her breast and scratched her pretty face with her nails,
and then, as she sank down on Parthenope's shore, she moaned,
and spoke the following words that were interrupted by sobbing:

Parthenope is the siren for whom the ancient site
of Naples was named. It's another literary flourish.
And Naples, of course, is the forest. The goats and lambs are people.
"Caliopus," as Boccaccio himself explained in a letter
is "good sound," or eloquence. "Pamphylus" is "loving all,"
and may be a mask for the author, troubled by the misfortunes
he describes. Calliope, the muse of epic, suggests
a hope of approaching that genre's grand historical sweep.
Chalcidia is the region from which the founders of Naples
came, so that here, the nymph bears that pertinent name.

"No forest in the world was happier or greater
or likelier to survive for endless ages than this,
in which the tall trees reached up to a kindly heaven,
beech and oak and ilex as well as cedar and cypress.
The Libistrian woods, teeming with bears, could not compare,
nor those in Ercinia, nurse to generations of heroes.

More froufrou. Libistria? In Africa somewhere,
but probably more important is its mention in the Aeneid.
Ercinia? It's Germany, but wearing lederhosen.
They're like the whipped cream we sometimes scrape from tops of sundaes.

Our forest was far better than that on Ida near Troy
where Paris made his fateful judgment, and better too
than the Berbycian wood or the Erymanthian. Here
were meadows full of flowers of yellow, violet, and pink
on which the light of Phoebus would shine in the early morning
so they glistened at least for a while with the diamonds of the dew.
We had clear springs that wandered among the grassy fields
and many fresh lakes that reflected the pale blue of sky.
We had our limestone caves that offered shepherds shelter.
We had our birds that twittered and called from their nests in the trees.
Parrots came from their distant habitat and the gorgeous
phoenix graced our groves, deigning to make its visit.
We had our roaring lions and our gentle deer and rabbits,
wild boars with their dangerous tusks, and bears of enormous strength.
Frolicking goats we had in abundance and fleecy sheep
with the best wool in the world. We had many herds of cattle
that chewed their cud in the shade and gave us milk and calves.
All that was back in the days of great Tityrus, who kept
the countryside in good order. Those days, alas, are gone.

Tityrus is King Roberto, il Saggio—no longer
Argus as before. We don't have to worry about it.

Ciclops" is Polyphemus, and refers to the same bad man,
Ludwig of Buda and Pest, who will shortly come on the scene.

Tityrus first sang the laws that were helpful and healthy for sheep,
and he was well known for his pastoral wisdom. (Alas, that fame
came to the ears of Ciclops to trouble his jealous heart.)
Under Tityrus we had another golden age
the equal of what the ancient shepherds described in their carvings
in the bark of the oldest oak trees. I remember how it was
when satyrs leapt and danced and nymphs wove flowered garlands.
The woods were alive with singing, and sounds of panpipes and strings
were everywhere. But why recall such wonderful times
that only underscore how much of that richness is gone?
Suffice it to say that the dizzying diminution is such
as one would find if he went from the oak to the tamarisk,
from the lofty cypress down to the lowly thornbush, or from
the alder down to the gray willow. It breaks my heart
to think of how much power Jove gives to the evil stars
and how Fortune can suddenly turn upon those she used to favor.
Weep, you men of the woods, weep bitter tears with me,
for the mighty oaks have fallen and the cypresses too are down.
Above the groves of ilex, smoke rises up from the fires
vandals have set, and the bare and blackened branches of pines
mark where they used to grow as living trees. The laurel
we think of as evergreen is a deathly white, and the myrtle's
branches are strewn on the ground. The soil is desert dry
in a vista that stretches away as far as the tearful eye
can see in the permanent murk. The singing birds are silent.
The shepherds' caves and cahoots are all destroyed, and the springs
are clotted with rotten moss. The banks of the rivers are fouled,
and ugly marsh reeds grow where wildflowers once blossomed.
What crimes could you have committed to deserve such retribution?
How could you or your fathers have offended the heavenly gods
to prompt them to such chastisement or invite so abrupt a decline?

These plagues from hell must have come to punish heinous sins
every bit as ghastly as this nightmare landscape,
beyond any description. O, you crude wood god
of fields and gardens for whom the privet and fair acanthus
used to bloom, can you see how your domain is reduced?
The figures of Priapus are supposed to ward off such ruin.
Were you sated with blossoming roses, bored with lilies and violets?
Have you developed a taste for dry brambles and thistles
instead of the succulent berries that appear in the summertime?
Hemlock now replaces that healthier vegetation
and the sedge that even the wild asses distrust and avoid.
Fauns and dryads, I ask you, how can we bear to see
the thickets we used to play in, dancing and singing, turned
to such a wasteland? The vines are gone from the tall elms
and the ivy is dry and dying. The golden fields have tarnished
to a moribund brown and the sparkling lakes and rivers are now
polluted so that fish—and the fishermen too—are gone.
The rotting hulls of their derelict boats litter the shore.
The sheep and goats are sick and their heartbroken herdsmen have fled.
The only healthy beasts are the predators that roam
what's left of the dwindling woodland. Even Alcestus has gone
with Liquoris, full of fear and loathing, sailing away
to someplace safe. Here only grief and worry flourish,
and beauty is no more. You ancient woodsmen, weep,
weep with me for the woods we loved, our woods that are dying,
and let us welcome death as our only remaining refuge."
That's what she said and then she sank down as if overcome.

Alcestus, of course, is Louis, and Liquoris is still Queen Joan.
The lament, which is convincing, comes from Boccaccio's heart.
He'd spent some time in Naples and loved the city. Florence?
For him it was mezzo mezz'. (Dante, off in Ravenna
had longed for it as he, in Florence, longed for Naples.)

PAMPHYLUS:

The poor dear! I think I can understand her complaint.
She hoped with her many tears to melt the stony hearts
of the spinning sisters and somehow undo some of the damage
foreseen by the gods. Alas, she is wrong in entertaining
so forlorn a hope. One must learn sooner or later
to yield to heaven's will. But did you not tell her this?
Did you not offer words of comfort as you would do to a mourner?

CALIOPUS:

I thought of it. I would have. But I was, I confess, afraid.
Could wicked Polyphemus hear of my attempt
to soothe her grief, what chance would I have to avoid his anger?
I came, instead, to you. You go and offer the comfort
of sympathetic words. She may listen perhaps to you.

PAMPHYLUS:

How can I thank you? How can I ever hope to repay you?
I'd offer you one of these beasts, but the flock isn't mine to give.
They all belong to my master. And Opheltes took my syrinx.
But Licisca has littered again, and when the puppies are done
nursing, you'll come to my house and pick any one you like.

CALIOPUS:

I will, and I thank you for it. Meanwhile, go to the girl,
and offer your sympathy and your love. She needs them now.
I have to go, I'm afraid. It's milking time for the sheep.

VI 🐚 Alcestus

AMINTAS:

The snow on the ground has melted, and the sheets of ice on the ponds
have broken up. The shepherds, happy to see this, play
songs of love on their pipes, as they always do in springtime.
They decorate their garlands of oak leaves with ivy vines,
set out bowls for Bacchus, and honor the god with singing,
performing the ancient rite. But you, Melibeus, mope,
and your unmistakable sadness hardly suits the season.

MELIBEUS:

The beautiful wood that Argus used to rule has fallen
into decay. It has crashed. His herdsmen have fled or perished.
Alcestus has taken his place, but we have no idea
where he may be found. Meanwhile a monster has come
to prey upon our sheepfolds and terrify our herds.

AMINTAS:

Have you not heard? Polyphemus, that monster to whom you refer,
has gone away! Alcestus is back. The wandering shepherds
have all returned to round up their scattered flocks as before.
The woods are green with joy and the hills and valleys echo
birdsongs of celebration. Auspicious stars in the sky
have risen above our meadows and the trees put forth new leaves

of hope and faith. The kids sprout little horns and butt
their carefree heads. The slopes of Mount Gaurus blossom,
and Vesuvius' grapes renew themselves in their sloping vineyards.
Falernus' elms revive. And Vulturnus' waters rush
in a babble of content. By its banks the shepherds pluck
their lyres and sing together of the welcome change in the weather.

King Ludwig has gone—perhaps in fear of the great plague,
or perhaps to prevent the Venetians from cutting him off from home.
"Alcestus" is still Louis, but new and improved, or at least
that's how he must have appeared in contrast to "Polyphemus."

MELIBEUS:
News like this is good, but sometimes hard to accept,
and we bite the gold coins Fortune lets us find on the road
to see if they're real. Old shepherds learn in time to be wary.
Divine Pan turned away from these woods he used to care for,
and it seemed that the heavens themselves had abandoned our Alcestus.
What birds of better omen have crossed our skies? What priest
has contrived to placate the gods and mollify their ire?
Go and put on your head the garlands of rejoicing,
but I shall stay here and continue my strains of lamentation,
which I have practiced enough to become quite a virtuoso.

AMINTAS:
Let fair Corrina never come again to my cave
if I am not telling the truth. The summit of Mount Cyrceus
shone with flames to mark Alcestus' longed-for return.
Garganus too and the mighty Appeninus were smoking
from their highest peaks in their celebration of what has happened.
Even Etna applauded in the only way volcanoes
can express emotion, mixing in with her black smoke
flashes of bright red flame. If you do not believe my words
then look around and believe the reports of your own senses

as you see the hillsides that turned a mournful brown reviving
to the customary green of vegetative health.
I swear to you that I saw him with my own eyes set foot
on Neapolitan soil and embrace his mother and sisters
in his loving arms and kiss them and receive in turn their kisses.

MELIBEUS:
My dear Amintas, your words are welcome to me as much
as the sun is welcome to flowers that droop from the night's long chill,
or as dittany is to goats, or rain to a parched field
thirsty from a prolonged spell of hot dry weather.

Dittany? That's what it says: "dictannus," something he knew
that was fun to throw in for its note of verisimilitude.
Virgil didn't know beans about farming—even growing
beans—he swotted it up from his Hesiod and took pride
in not having any firsthand knowledge. Boccaccio knew
at least this single fact, and it was pleasing to make
his shepherd sound like a shepherd. Related to marjoram,
it has woolly, weak stems, thick leaves, and pinkish flowers,
is native to Greece, and is sometimes used as an herb in cooking.

To you, O Lord Apollo, we pray for your grace and favor,
and to you, O fruitful Pales, goddess of pastures and sheepfolds,
we offer thanks and plead that you may treat us kindly.

Clear enough, but the way they thought back then could allow
for divinities, male and female, to suggest Jesus and Mary.
It doesn't insist, but then it doesn't exclude it either.

I cannot remember so fine a day dawning for shepherds.
Phorba, go and erect some earthen altars for us.
Put them near water, and hang them with ivy and myrtle leaves.
Bring as well some palm fronds and lead in a snowy ram

for sacrifice to let the gods know we are thankful.
Make sure that you do it right. And you, Lycrophron, go
and see that the flock is fed and watered. Then you can play
your pipes for them and for us. It was a hard winter,
but now that spring has come, we ought to rejoice and sing.
And Amintas, you and I should visit the holy shrines.
You will deck yourself with olive leaves, and I
shall wear a garland of poplar as you play the sacred tunes,
and I shall sing secundo. We are a first-rate duo,
as good, I think, as any you'll find in Sicily—
except of course for Yollas, whose music is almost divine.
He is like a cypress that towers over us briars.

Yollas is almost certainly Petrarch, who used to be
Mopsus: but why worry? The point of these shepherd costumes
is how transparent they are—as they were with Virgil, too.

AMINTAS:
Yes, by all means, my friend. It is right and proper to sing
songs of celebration. But you must begin the music,
for you have the better voice. Sing, perhaps, of Phyllis,
whose name you once incised high in the bark of an oak
with a long-handled rake. Sing of that or of any love,
all those we have ever known or imagined. Sing
of life, which is the aim and result of love. Or sing
of Alcestus, who gives us back our lives. What trials he endured
with Phytias! You've heard the praises of Stilbon's verses?
Let us endorse and expand on the themes of that man's work!

Stilbon is one of Mercury's names (it occurs in Ovid)
but here it refers to Zanobi da Strada, the court poet
of Naples—and also a friend of Niccola Acciaiuoli,
the seneschal whose label is "Phytias." All clear?

MELIBEUS:

Ah, sweet Phyllis, may she romp in the meadows forever!
And Phytias, let him pursue the successes of his career
as Jove looks down on him with approval and satisfaction.
It's Alcestus whom we should praise and give thanks to in our music,
for he will establish peace and an order in which we can live
the harmonious lives we've dreamt of with ever-diminishing hopes.
Let the Muses raise our songs to the stars above
whose configurations at last are omens of good tidings.

AMINTAS:

Look at us, man! We sit in the tranquil shade together
as the altars are set up that will please the benevolent gods.
Our flocks are chewing the cud in a season that gives us hope.
What better time could there be than this for songs and verses?

MELIBEUS:

I think of the harsh Fates that beset us and drew Alcestus
from his accustomed woodlands. The nymphs were weeping. Naples
mourned and all Apulia suffered. Bacchus drank
until he was senseless, as sheep and heifers sickened and died.
The Vulturnus ignored its banks and scattered rocks and mud
in fields plowmen had worked. Mountains were veiled with smoke,
and fog filled every valley. At night there were howls of beasts
as if the entire countryside had gone into mourning.
The lions of the land were hushed and were caught in traps
set by the wicked hunters. The lynxes' eyesight failed.

*Lions? Well, not exactly. They are the princes, and Ludwig
is the wicked hunter. The traps of course would be his prisons.*

Fortune seemed vindictive as it bore down upon us, relentless,
with every kind of misfortune. O Phoebus, jewel of the sky,
I pray to you and thank you for having deigned to end

Alcestus' bitter troubles and restore him at last to his woods.
May all the nymphs and fauns, shepherds and farm boys sing
your praises now and forever, for giving us light and life.

AMINTAS:
Thyme is not more pleasing to buzzing bees, nor hibiscus
to lambs, nor clover to goats, than is your song to me.
Allow me a variation upon your splendid theme.
  You hills, you mountains, applaud, for Alcestus has returned
and now is among us to lead us. Let the waves roar in approval,
and the shore resound with its gasps of relief and gratitude.
Alcestus has turned his attention from earth to the sun and stars,
all in their orderly orbits, and the rising and setting moon.
Astrea, goddess of justice, who also was driven away,
he has called back and now, with her help, he can yoke his car
with bulls. He can reconcile the deer and the lion or wolves
with sheep in their folds. He can rid the farmers' furrows of snakes.
He will support the Muses and honor those who serve them.
  You hills, you mountains, applaud, for Alcestus has returned.
He has come home and as long as fish live in the water,
or four-footed beasts wander the woods and meadows, or birds
soar and swoop in the air, or stars revolve in the skies,
so long may Alcestus remain among us, the light
and life of the forest, the shepherds' wise guide and protector.
May he never see the dark doors of Dis agape
but rise like the sun to take his place among heaven's gods.
  You hills, you mountains, applaud, for Alcestus has returned.
He has come home again. It is right that we celebrate.
Let us slaughter a lamb and let Alcestus see this.
And for him? A spotless bull should be led to the gods' altar,
while he presides, his brow decked with a laurel garland.
On that happy day we will leap and dance in our leather buskins.
Asylas, the talented Tuscan, will sound his pipes, and Damon
and Phytias will stand before him singing his praise.

Phytias is still Acciaiuoli. The other two?
There aren't even guesses. But certainly they are friends.

You hills, you mountains, applaud, for Alcestus has returned.
He has come home again. It is right that we celebrate.
Those who come after us will scarcely believe the reports
that they will read inscribed in the bark of the tallest trees—
the hazel, poplar, and beech—of your many noble deeds.
Your name will remain alive in the hearts of our descendants
as long as the Po flows, as long as the mountains give shade
to the valleys, as long as hibiscus and willow grow that the goats
adore. The Arno will have to acknowledge and praise your deeds.

In Florence, you will remember, they turned Louis away.
And Boccaccio wasn't happy living there. Ergo,
he wasn't displeased to have this chance to cock a snook.

You hills, you mountains, applaud, for Alcestus has returned.
He has come home again. It is right that we celebrate.

MELIBEUS:
What a splendid song! I cannot imagine what prizes
you and it deserve. As myrtles are to brambles,
as balsam is to broom, or laurel leaves to seaweed,
so much do you surpass Menalcas, I declare,
with your elegant turns and tropes. You rise to Yollas' heights
and his pipes can move stones. What present can I give you
to show my admiration? I have one fine possession
that the Spartan Ylas made. There were two drinking vessels
but lovely Phyllis has one. I will give you the other,
a simple perfect thing that no one's lips have touched.

AMINTAS:
I take it as more than a prize for singing, for it is a token
of friendship—the value of which even Yollas would acknowledge.
I beg you, in return, to accept from me a staff
that Lycidas once gave me. It came from Camander's cliff
where, as a youth, he used to hunt the Phrygian deer.
It is gnarled with attractive knots and it has a tip of gold.
    But I heard a noise just now. Did you? Listen a moment!
Yes, I do hear barking. One of them is Melampus,
and the other, I am sure, is Licisca. They are warning
that something is wrong. A wolf is nosing about the sheepfold
or some other savage beast. I must go there at once.
Come along with me, would you? I may need your help.

The wolf is probably Ludwig, whose troops have not yet withdrawn,
or it could be Charles IV, who in 1354
crossed the Alps so he could receive the Lombard crown
in Milan (in which he stayed only a matter of hours).
But it doesn't matter. The point is that troubles are probably coming,
which isn't a far-fetched prediction, either then or now.

VII 🐚 The Quarrel

DAPHNIS:

You snore the afternoon away. You neglect your sheep.
You could have asked me to look after them, but, no,
you just lie there and drowse, having drunk so much wine.
What can you say for yourself? What excuse do you have?

FLORIDA:

Are you any better, Daphnis? Why would I ask a thief
to guard my flock? And you are not always sober, either.

Daphnis, Mercury's son, was the first shepherd, and here
the name applies to the emperor, Charles IV. The other,
Florida, is Florence. The quarrel between these two
was worrisome to Boccaccio, who had gone to Avignon,
representing Florence, to learn of the pope's intentions.
If the emperor came to Rome, the power of Florence and Naples
would both be much diminished. This is the quarrel's subject.

DAPHNIS:

Don't get high-hat with me. You think I didn't see you
emerging from Phaselis' sheepfold the other night,
with one hand holding a sheep you'd stolen and, with the other,
combing your mussed up tresses. What would Lupiscus think?

Who are all these people? Phaselis stands for Lucca,
which Florence wants to take back. The Visconti family had it
but then sold it to Pisa. Lupiscus is very likely
one of the house of Visconti. The sheep are the ones you fleece,
which is to say the people who happen to live in these cities.

FLORIDA:
It was my ram in the first place. I was just taking it back.
You are the one who's a thief. I saw you myself, near Pisa,
rustling sheep and goats and none to careful about it.
Phaselis was crying out, but that didn't faze you. You ran,
dragging the poor beasts through dense and thorny thickets.

DAPHNIS:
You lie! Those were my own sheep I was taking to market.
Don't I have the right to do with them as I please?

FLORIDA:
You might, if only for courtesy's sake, try to make your lies
plausible. What you've just said is arrant nonsense!
What outlandish wind blew into your ear to addle
your tiny brain. You, your father, and his father
—if indeed you know who they are—are savages all.
"My own," has a meaning here other than what you can hold
in your arms as you run away from the man whom you've just robbed.

DAPHNIS:
What will fair Galathea say when she hears your words?
You sound like ugly Lusca, whom I expect to insult me.
The older farmers around these parts have learned to trust me
and have put me in charge of their sheep and all their grassy pastures.

Galathea is Rome and "Lusca," which means one-eyed,
refers to Milan, which is the Viscontis' seat of power.

They trust in my good judgment, and the sheepfolds I protect
extend as far as the Indus and Hebrus in rocky Thrace
all the way to the African deserts. You crazy woman,
your farcical attempts to condescend to me
are pathetic and bizarre. I begin to lose my patience.

FLORIDA:
You begin to lose more than that. Think of all those who have died
and gone to heaven or hell, whom you were supposed to protect.
Scarcely a corner of these great woods is truly yours
or pays any attention to your fragile decrees. Your rule
is notional at best, for the Moselle's current does not
reach the Indian plain, nor the Rhine's flow extend
to the African sands. The titles you claim from all these places
are honorific at best, and the world tries to hide its grin
when you and your foolish friends are brazen enough to use them.

DAPHNIS:
What backs them up is my pack of fine Molossian hounds
that circle about me and snarl and show the world their teeth.

Molossian hounds? They are, by bucolic convention, his soldiers.
They came from near Epirus, and according to legend, Laeleps,
the first of these, was forged by Heaphestus and cast in bronze.
He gave it breath and a soul and presented it to Zeus.
There are still Molossoid breeds: the Rottweiler, the Boxer,
the Neapolitan mastiff, the Boerboel, the Ca de Bou.
You get the idea. They're large—attack dogs, guard dogs, and fighters.

Even now, Galathea is saving laurel branches
with which some day she hopes to adorn my head. And you
laugh at my titles? I think you'll wish soon enough you hadn't.

FLORIDA:

Galathea will deck your hair with garlands of laurel
when pigs fly, when burning torches put out fires,
when the rising sun brings darkness. Those who have been so honored
would throw their laurel chaplets in rage and shame to the pigs
if they should see you wear that insignia, undeserved
and utterly absurd. I'd rather go blind or die
than see someone like you strutting around in laurel.

DAPHNIS:

You're aware, are you not, that you're raving? Do you dare defy
Apollo's decrees? A better and much more prudent plan
would have been for you to accept the truth of the world as it is
and offer your flowers to add to my laurel leaves so that Jove
might watch your flocks from above and protect them from wolves and
    foxes.

You may perhaps remember that, earlier, "Lupiscus"
signified a member of the house of Visconti. "Lupus"
means wolf, and therefore the passage alludes to the plea that Florence
had made to Charles for his protection against Milan.
Charles refused to involve himself, and his patronizing
offer would have appeared to readers in Florence, false,
not quite a joke perhaps, but more than a little sardonic.

FLORIDA:

I have been paying attention for years and I can see
through to your tricky and timorous heart. You use the snare
rather than hunt game with a spear that you're not good at.
You think a few flattering words to me would be like bait
to draw me into your trap, but I am not blind or stupid.
Once I would have conceded to you the entire forest,
all the sheep and goats and bulls and cows. No more!
And no more embraces and kisses. Those times are gone forever

when Daphnis looked important, a great man at the crossroads.
You claim that it is Apollo who tells you to deck your head
with the sacred laurel, but I just don't believe you. The heavens,
Golia says, were given to gods, but the earth to men.
I take this to mean that each man or woman can choose
how to behave. I am free. I was never joined to a husband.
I renounced the marriage bed and answer to no one else.
My spirits are high, and my strength has never yet failed me.
I have my bow and arrows and my pack of rough sheepdogs
that wild Licisca bore. I tell you I'd rather die
before I let go of my lilies or throw them to the crows.

The lily, an old symbol of Florence, appeared on the florin.
And the crows? As a matter of fact, they are purely and simply crows.

DAPHNIS:
You may not be married, but I have seen for myself how many
adulterers you've welcomed into your unmade bed.
Phaselis' marshy ground still shows their footprints' path.
You pay for your guards with cash and therefore what you get
are the dregs of men, escaped prisoners, runaway slaves,
none of whom are disciplined fighters, or brave, or loyal,
but desperadoes and fugitives, fleeing us and our woods.
The lot of them aren't worth an arrow from my quiver,
but rather the whips and cudgels that are more than enough to drive them
to instant flight. You should go back to women's work,
spinning, weaving, and sewing, and leave the fields to farmers.
Cultivate your garden, grow your kitchen herbs,
tend your flower beds, and gather roses and violets
for garlands for your girls. Slaughter your fat hogs
and prepare a feast for your household. Encourage some of your sons
to comb their beards, dress up, put garters on their thighs,
and let them preen by the smooth pools that show their reflections,
but flatter so that they seem to be slender rather than pudgy.

Give them all reed pipes and provide them with shady dells
in which to loll and play. Bring on the brazen nymphs
and let the good wine flow. Drive the noisy cicadas
out of the trees and shoo off the packs of barking dogs
so that nothing may disturb their pleasant postprandial naps.
Never mind what you do to their character and morale,
making them ever more wretched. The Phrygian shepherd mocked me,
and Osyris dared to show me his sneers of derisive contempt,
but they did not go unpunished, and neither, I think, will you.

The Phrygian shepherd? The pope. It's Innocent VI.
And Osyris? This is code for the house of Visconti, whose emblem
was—and maybe still is—a serpent. Yes, it's a reach,
but this is a game and the far-fetched associations are fun.

FLORIDA:
I will do as you say, enjoying the sweet springtime
when the woods are serene and the gentle breezes tousle the leaves,
at least in part so that you may be troubled with pangs of envy.
You accuse me of love affairs, but who do you think will believe you?
Dirty old men like you often accuse chaste matrons
of what they would do themselves if only they still could.
Jove's mighty oak is my witness. What you have said is as false
as your own threats and boasts. You talk of the Phrygian shepherd
and bandy about the name of Osyris. The sorry truth
is rather different. Despite your empty claims of conquest
I know you have never ventured into Canopus' forests,
or the far-off Mysian hills, or Camander's rocky valleys.
If a big bird picked you up and dropped you down in these places,
would you recognize terrain that you'd never seen before?

Canopus is in Egypt, and therefore means the Visconti
holdings. Camander, meanwhile, and the Mysian hills are the pope's

"Phrygian" territories. Charles was the emperor,
but the Milanese had the men and the power and called the tune.

You'll sing these songs, I am sure, to the innocent nymphs who dwell
along the Danube, and maybe some of them will believe you.
But also sing of the door with the serpent carved on its face,
and the iron crown that was splotched with rust, the emblem of shame,
because of the great reluctance you showed in Venice's fields.

The door with the serpent? The gate of Milan through which Charles
       entered
with only a minimal escort. He had to watch the parade
of Visconti strength. He was crowned and then, in a matter of hours,
ended his visit and fled, as if from a prison cell.
The rusty crown, bestowed in 1355,
alludes to Charles' response to the Lombards' invitation
that the emperor should join them in fighting against the Visconti—
the Lombard states and Venice, together against Milan.
But even then, poor Charles was lacking in will or nerve.

Before you make any threats, it would be well to erase
those shameful associations that most of us still have.
You warn that you will destroy the sheepfolds, the oaks, and the beeches,
but we laugh at you. We defy you. What you should do is go
to your home at the end of the earth and put up a safe fort
for the women and children. You can catch wild asses and try
to tame them. You and your servants can trim back some of your vines
that are in great need of tending. That ought to keep you busy.

DAPHNIS:
It's tiresome to argue with stupid croaking frogs!
I'm sorry for your children, who have learned to comb your hair,
wash your face, and get you dressed in the mornings. You hear
their fulsome praise, in which you seem now to believe.

But the Arno will carry the news to its mouth and tell the Pisans
how I will place the heel of my boot on your stringy neck
and empty your wretched guts of their last drops of blood.

FLORIDA:
Hercules, the hero of Tyrins, gave me the golden
apples he said can bring deep sleep to feverish men.
These I will use to calm your fulminating rages,
and the Milanese will wake you from your fantastic dreams.

*The golden apples represent the 100,000
florins the Florentines paid to Charles to leave them alone.
But beyond the money, Florence relies on the Milanese
of whom Charles is afraid, and not without good reason.*

VIII ❧ Midas

DAMON:

Get your sheep out of here! Don't you know where you are?
I warn you, Phytias, Midas, if he should see them here,
will rush out to attack them, or, just as likely, take them
himself and guard them. This holds for Lupisca, too.

Identifications, maybe, are useful here. Our Damon
is likely to be Maghinardo dei Cavalcanti, a friend
from Florence who, in Naples, invited the poet to stay
as a guest in his house, Boccaccio having been disgraced
at court. Midas, who shares his name with the Phrygian king,
is an avaricious person—Niccola Acciaiuoli.
And Lupisca is perhaps his sister Andrea,
who was wife and mother of two conspirators who killed
Prince Andrew and therefore might have played a part in that crime.
Niccola's other sister was Lupa, whose real name
is rather closer. Still, my money would be on the other.

PHYTIAS:

What are you saying, my friend? You insult these prominent people!
What motive would they possibly have for such behavior?
They used to be poor when Midas guarded his master's sheep
and Lupisca spent her nights at Minerva's task, weaving.

But look at them now! Aufidus tends their herds of cows
and a Marsian servant takes the calves from their mothers' udders.
I do not come as a foe. Midas himself invites me.
He will provide me, I'm sure, with pastureland for my flock,
with a brook, I daresay, and trees that offer their cooling shade.

Acciaiuoli invited Boccaccio to Naples
in 1355 and 1362.
Neither visit went well, and Boccaccio's resentment
is the subject of this eclogue. That's how writers get even.

DAMON:
Gather your sheep together and, while you still can, flee.
Bitter weather is coming and you'll wish you had never come.
Promises are easy, but they float off into the air
more often than we'd like to admit to ourselves. Their flocks
are large—but ask yourself how they accumulated
such an enormous number. You know what honest work
can produce. But by foul play one can do, in the short run,
very much better than that. They're suspiciously successful.

PHYTIAS:
Good grief! It appears that I have, yet again, been duped.
Where shall I find a tranquil place to lay my head?
Where can I take my sheep to let them graze in safety?
There was nothing wrong with the pastures back home. The rivers and
    streams
had not run dry. I swear what brought me here to the south
was trust in what I took to be their kindness and hope
that I might prosper here. But you tell me of Midas' greed
and Lupisca's cruel behavior. I ought to have been more careful
and should have looked before I leapt. But I am here
beside Vesuvius' heights and Gaurus' emerald bay.
Tell me, if you would, those truths I need to know

to protect myself. It's winter. No little birds are likely
to give me this information. What is it that they do
to seize these flocks and herds? How do they manage this?

DAMON:
It starts off with a nymph, as these things often do,
the jewel of the forest whose husband suddenly passed away.
Midas was coming to market with cheeses he'd made from sheep milk
and skins of those he'd slaughtered. He saw the nymph and burned
with instant ardor. That day, on his way back home, his pockets
were full of money. Some say he gave her a gift and then
made love to her, though others insist that he simply raped her
and the gift was an afterthought, an attempt to keep her quiet.
But whichever way it happened, she was now his captive—
as he was hers, for she was both highborn and lovely.
Then Argus died, and then Alexis soon thereafter
perished one way or another. Midas seized the moment,
starting fraternal quarrels, intriguing in shepherds' affairs
and sewing seeds of discord wherever they might be useful.

The nymph is almost surely Caterina di Courtenay,
Filippo di Taranto's widow (he was the brother
of King Roberto, or "Argus"). Acciaiuoli was rumored
to be Caterina's lover, and the money from cheeses and skins
stands for what he borrowed (or, putting it bluntly, embezzled)
from his banking firm. "Alexis" still stands for Prince Andrew.

Midas arranged the marriage of Ametus to Melalces,
and in return demanded garlands to put on his brow
and an oaken staff to carry, and the lofty titles of gods,
even though, until then, his name had been quite unknown.

"Ametus" is code for Louis, who was Caterina's son
and Acciaiuoli's pupil. Melalces is Queen Joan.

This match required a special papal dispensation
because it was widely believed that Joan had taken part
in Andrew's murder. The poet may even be implying
that Acciaiuoli had a hand in that crime himself.

PHYTIAS:

It must have taken a lot of nerve along with luck
for a man who was just a servant to trump himself up that way.

DAMON:

You're not getting it, are you? He made his own good luck
getting on as he did with nymphs and fauns of the wood,
while keeping his eyes open for sheep and goats he could steal
from no matter whom. His greatest advantage was that he was not
fettered at all by any conventional moral constraints.

PHYTIAS:

Still, it seems to me that if Jupiter had not wanted
the man to rise to such high honors, it wouldn't have happened.

DAMON:

Is it Phytias who stands before me? Or have you changed
to Lycurgus of ancient Sparta with all this pious piffle?
Look around you and see these rich sulfurous hills
where the vines have always grown so well. Our great lord Bacchus
has promoted a mere swineherd—and it has to be a joke.

PHYTIAS:

I'm Phytias, your old friend. The same poor shepherd, I fear,
and I've learned how to soothe my goats and to entertain myself,
playing the pipes of Pan. What I have not yet learned
are the ways of men and how they behave when they live in cities.
I've heard Lycurgus' name, but I couldn't tell you a thing
about his life or work. I'm a shepherd, for heaven's sake.

And you ought not to mock me or make me the butt of your snide
    remarks.
Apollo gave you a lyre, and Pomona, the goddess of fruit trees,
gave you an orchard with branches bowed down with their ripening fruits.
But now that you have attained such heights of success and comfort,
do not look down with contempt at those who have not yet risen
or those who have fallen back. Amintas, our old companion,
has often sung, you remember, of Fortune's fickle whims.
We live a life of tears that only our deaths will end.

Amintas, you may remember, was one of the two speakers
in an earlier eclogue. The name makes no particular reference
to any writer outside the putative countryside.

DAMON:
Get hold of yourself, man. Things could be lots worse.
Boats will make their wakes across the blue skies before
Damon abandons Phytias; chariot wheels will leave
their tracks in the waves, and dolphins will play on the mountaintops,
before our friendship fails. Whatever comes, we'll face it
together as comrades. But you must come to your senses and see
the facts before your eyes that can't be ignored or denied.
He used to come like some sly beast, sneak through the grass,
grab nanny goats by their tails and savage their helpless kids.
Then he grew stronger and took on larger aims and targets.
He was a bull that tears at the vetch with his sharp curved horn
and then knocks down tall pines and uproots mighty oaks,
filling the whole forest with a fearsome bellowing. He
was a lion terrifying the oxen and prompting the growling
bears to lumber away as fast as their bodies could move,
crashing through the brush. From Bevies' pens the shameless
man took goats and cows and he led fat bulls from their stalls
while Melampus barked himself hoarse. How many fauns and nymphs
did he deceive! How many gullible satyrs from distant

hillsides did he cozen! He puts on a good show
and has managed to fool himself. Now he has taken on airs
as if he were a new Maecenas, almost a god.
He's a patron now of the arts, and he's rounded up the Muses
he keeps high on a cliff as if they were his possessions.

It wasn't the muses themselves. He tried to recruit Petrarch
as the court poet of Naples. When Petrarch turned him down
he settled upon Zanobi da Strada—whose name does not
resonate. He also invited Boccaccio down
but then treated him badly. Boccaccio wrote to a friend
describing Acciaiuoli as a man who would talk about books
pretending that he had read them. We all know people like that.

He thinks that his voice resounds as Hesiod's once did
and his singing can move the forests, the gods, and the sacred sisters
to approach him the better to hear his demisemiquavers.
The truth is, he's a tyrant who destroys the woods and meadows,
preys on cattle and men—and his sister even worse.
Lupisca takes the husks from pigs, the grass from lambs,
and steals calves from their mothers. She shears her sheep too often
and milks them three times a day. She uses whatever black magic
she knows to cast her spells on other men's goats and kids.
Her greed and lust are such that she busies herself all night
when you see her on Mount Guarus rushing by in the moonlight.
She leaves nothing untouched, unsullied, or undisturbed
and leads young boys astray luring them into her caves
where she strips them naked and teaches extravagant perversions.

PHYTIAS:
I have no idea what to say! Midas a common thief?
And his sister is a miser, magician, and harlot, too?
Not very long ago she was gathering fallen acorns

and gleaning from olive trees what little remained after harvest.
Now she's become a blemish on earth and an outrage to heaven.
What has Melalces said, or her husband Ametus? Nothing?

DAMON:
They have been silent, which people interpret as consent.
Some say that the gods permit the depredations of Midas
as punishment for the murder of poor unavenged Alexis.

PHYTIAS:
I am sorry to have come here. I've made an awful mistake.
These pastures I took to be so welcoming and rich
have turned, as if a cloud had come across the sky,
dark, so that they seem full of danger and threaten harm.
It was never my purpose to come and pretend that brambles were bays
or praise to the heavens a man who turns out not to be worthy.
Swineherds are not divine, however they trick themselves out.
I was deceived as you tell me so many others have been.
I'm a poor man but not so destitute as to turn
to flattery and fawning. Before I left home, I heard
a crow on a branch of an ancient oak give me warning
that the auguries for my journey were grim. I did not listen,
but hope and desire beguiled me and led me down here to fields
that are tainted with evil and menace. Before Coridon came here
he used to sing cheerful songs underneath the laurels' shelter.

Coridon is Zanobi da Strada, who came to Naples
in 1352. He worked for Niccola's brother,
Angelo Acciaiuoli, the Bishop of Monte Cassino.
Niccola then crowned him as the laureate of Naples.
Boccaccio says of him that he wrote mediocre verse
(and maybe had a sexual relation with Niccola too).

DAMON:

You cannot begin to imagine how Coridon has changed.
He plays his songs on a pipe I'd just as soon not describe.
He's a different man from the one you knew who used to play
his tunes out in the fields when he set his traps for game.

PHYTIAS:

What do I do, Damon? Should I try to tough it out?
Or should I flee this dismal and unprepossessing shore?

DAMON:

Remember what the plowboys of the good old days would say?
It was good advice back then. It's good, and it's relevant, now.

PHYTIAS:

I'd rather live in a simple hut in a wooded wasteland
and let my sheep lick the barren stones of Mount Lycaeus
than graze on the rich soil of Stymphalian meadowland,
inviting but full of danger, as poor travelers learned.

*Lycaeus is the home of Pan, an Arcadian mountain,
and Stymphalia is where Hercules killed the vicious birds.*

Beneath some sheltering cliff in safety will I sing
with Amiclas, my friend, or even, if we are lucky,
the splendid Silvanus, whose songs can calm a troubled mind,
turning wrath and lust to a cheerful tranquility.

*Silvanus is Petrarch. Boccaccio, on his way back from Naples
in 1363, visited him. The other,
Amiclas, could be Barbato da Sulmona,
on whom he also dropped in during that same journey.*

DAMON:
What could be better than that? The last time I washed my sheep
each eddy in the water seemed to me to whirl
in a strange way. I read it as foretelling mighty storms.
In the fury of one of these our Midas could easily topple
and his sheep could be destroyed. Lupisca could fall
and be reduced to grubbing again on the ground for acorns.
These things happen. Whatever those two worry about
the rest of us can hope for. Meanwhile, you can hide.
Off in our remote regions are flowering meadows
and hidden caves I know that are pleasing to nymphs and fauns.
Your friend Glaucus can strew the floor with fragrant leaves
and prepare you her honeycombs. Come with me. I'll show you.
You'll see the trailing arbutus spreading out in the shadows.
They're what we have to look for. They cover the mouth of the cave.

PHYTIAS:
Lead the way. I'll follow. Let Lupisca be damned.

IX   Anxiety

BATRACOS:

You're a stranger here in these woods. May I know your name, sir?

ARCHAS:

I was an Arcadian once, where I lived on a mountain.
I come by chance to these shores where I live now. My name
is Archas. I see all around fat herds and thriving flocks,
but not much pastureland in your barren and stony fields.

Get it? Well, of course not. It's a joke, the point of which
demands too much information for it to be still funny.
"Batracos" is Greek for frog. It isn't the French,
who are "frogs" because they eat the legs of those creatures, sautéed,
but the Florentines, who Boccaccio thought were noisy and timid.
As frogs. Even back then it didn't get big guffaws.
Archas is just a stranger, although perhaps he picked
the name because it sounds like Arcadia, where he comes from.
The fat herds and flocks are the prosperous men of Florence.

BATRACOS:

It's a paradox but it's true. But unless you have pressing business,
come in and rest a while. We can entertain each other.
Tell me, to begin with, what is your journey's purpose?

ARCHAS:

You are most kind. I have myself often welcomed strangers
and invited them to sit with me in the shade of the trees.
Apollo approves of men who are hospitable—like you.
But tell me about the herds and flocks and how they thrive.

BATRACOS:

There are, not too far away, rich pastures where they graze
watered by streams and full of succulent grasses. There
they go in the mornings, trotting along together more briskly
than cattle often go. And then, by themselves, in the evenings,
they return home with their swollen udders they offer their calves
in order that they may nurse and grow in strength and size.

ARCHAS:

That's splendid. You seem to have very clever sheep and cows.
But you asked what brings me here. I have come to see Amarillis.

Amarillis is Rome. Virgil uses the same
name to designate that city in Eclogue I.

BATRACOS:

What do they know in Arcadia of our Amarillis, I wonder?

ARCHAS:

Who on earth has not heard of the famous Amarillis?

BATRACOS:

But tell me, friend, what have you to do with Amarillis?
You Dorians and you people from Thrace are not involved
with the care of sacred things and you scorn our holy altars.

ARCHAS:
There are some who say that Circius will come to claim the honors
that were given in ancient times to athletes and sometimes to poets.
I came to see the ceremony, to watch as they wreathed his head
with the laurel leaves. And then, having come all that way,
I thought I could learn a little—of how they cultivate fields,
how they tend their flocks and herds, and how they make cheese,
as well as their rites and customs and the laws in this part of the woods.

Circius is the name of a wind that blows from the north
and therefore refers to Charles IV, the Bohemian king
who also comes from the north. And they both begin with C.

BATRACOS:
This must be the reason for the mountain peaks in the Alps
to be emitting unusual smoke. It also explains
why the wolf with the suckling twins is barking. Foxes snuffle
and frighten the crowing roosters. The Rutulian shepherds groan
all through the night, afraid of every moving shadow.
Ferns may now offer cinnamon; Corsican yews may drip
with balsam; and the dreaded hemlock may offer up
rich Sabaean perfumes—if Romans approve of this rite.

The wolf is Rome, and the roosters are probably kings of France.
(But who, then, are the foxes?) Rutulians are Romans
dressed up as ancients and therefore quaint and picturesque.

ARCHAS:
You speak with some indignation. You're troubled by Circius' prospects?
What would you say to his face if he were here in person?

BATRACOS:
Why would I change my tune? I am distressed to see
how chance has been adverse to the settled ways of the world,
putting Italian laurels on tonsures of men of the north.

ARCHAS:
Italian laurels are mostly able to satisfy
the butting kids. But are they better than what you'd find
at beautiful Sirmio up on the shores of the Garda Lake.

Butting kids? They must be petty Italian leaders,
undertaking their mostly harmless skirmishes.
Why Sirmio is mentioned, I haven't the vaguest idea.

BATRACOS:
Archas, my friend, remember the laurel's glorious past
and how Phoebus Apollo awarded those leaves to men
victorious with their quivers or lyres. He loved the laurel,
into which his Daphne had turned to elude his grasp.
For that reason, the ancients used it for badges of honor.

ARCHAS:
What kinds of splendid deeds did they recognize in this way?

BATRACOS:
It's a long and very distinguished list. Unless I go on
for hours, I can only offer a few examples
of the kinds of achievements that used to deserve the gift of laurel
for you to carry back to your friends on the sacred mountain.
   Linternus withdrew the poisons the Libyan plague had brought
to our Ausonian farmland and made them spread their sickness
back in their own hills. He also introduced
splendid Falernian honey to delight our simple palates,
and better rules that he compelled all men to obey.

Linternus, the name of Scipio's villa, refers to him,
while the Libyan plagues are invasions of Carthage—the Punic Wars.
Ausonian farmland? Italian territory, puffed up,
the Ausoni, of course, being an ancient Italic tribe.

Rustic Arpinas plowed the Cyrthean mountains and sailed
his flock of smelly goats up the River Tiber,
where he tamed the Cimbrian bulls and broke into bits the gaudy
chariots that somehow they had been trained to draw.

More code. Arpinas is "rustic," because Marius was a plebeian.
He gained fame for subduing the Cimbrians and Teutons.

Opheltes was even faster than any Hyrcanian tigers
and he was the one to put down the savage Armenian lions
as well as the shaggy camels in Syrian caravans.
He carried off the Assyrian flocks and those that grazed
on the shores of the Red Sea in vessels that brought them here
to the shadows Tarpeia casts. He seized the Cilicians' ships
and took their proud prows and their oars as his people's trophies.

Opheltes has to be Pompey, whose great successes in Asia
Boccaccio mentions here albeit with gongoristic
embellishments. Tarpeia's rock is in Rome, and the flocks
are prisoners of war on display in his parade.

By his valor, Daphnis placed halters upon the fierce
Allobrogian bulls and the Aeduan as well.
He roped the Belgian calves and disciplined their weary
shepherds and cowherds that wandered through the misty mountains
altogether carefree. They lowered their necks to his yoke.

Daphnis? Julius Caesar. The bulls and calves and the herdsmen
are all transalpine Gauls. Remember? "In partes tres . . ."?

And the young Corigillus cut off the feet of the Hyperborean
griffins, the claws of which had been scratching the peaceful calves
that graze in fields along the banks of the mighty Hyster.

Patience, patience. It's almost over. This Corigillus
is the Claudius Drusus, who later on came to be known
as Germanicus, a general in Tiberius' army. He fought
Pannonians and Germans. The Hyster is the Danube.

There is of course the man from Smyrna and there is the shepherd
from Venice as well as the great Etruscan who long ago
with the tunes of their excellent reeds managed to tame the wild
Maeonian bullocks, Italy's lions, and Tyrian boars.

These are poets. The man who came from Smyrna is Homer.
Virgil is the Venetian. The Etruscan is either Dante
or less likely but still possibly Petrarch. The point
of the litany is that these are the men who are truly worthy
of wearing the laurel crown. Zanobi da Strada is not
anywhere in this league. (He, you will recall,
is the laureate now in Naples.) Boccaccio is not pleased,
and the long list is therefore an elaborate put-down,
an extended joke—and also a way of showing off,
keeping up the pastoral pretense, although just barely.

But why go on? You've surely understood what I mean.
The man who took the apples of the Hesperides and led
Hiberian cows home to Latium and took
the Briton's hides, or he who took the Phrixian fleece
from faraway Colchis . . . They clearly earned the right to mount
those alabaster chariots of Jupiter, to receive
the people's fervent applause for what they had done, and to crown
their brows with the consecrated garlands of laurel leaves.

These aren't so difficult. They are Hercules and Jason.

ARCHAS:
Theirs are all great achievements, worthy of being retold
again and again. But why do you seem so exercised?
Descendants can surely deserve what their forefathers had to earn.
And if we accept that theory, Circius has merit.

BATRACOS:
On that theory or any other that one might imagine,
it is difficult to see how a worthless layabout
like him should deserve our honors. His ancestors? Who were they?
They came with their crude axes to cut down Latium's forests.
They were hostile to Latian sheep with their huge Molossian hounds.
My mother was being foolish when she yielded laurels to him!

The convention is that the city of Rome is the mother of Florence.

Terrible things happen that heaven either permits
or deliberately inflicts as a reprimand. We recall
how the one-eyed shepherd came to slaughter our sheep with his sword
and burn our caves with Byrsian fire . . . and even then,
in the face of such grave danger, the leaders would not consent
that one of the two chief shepherds of the perishing flock should be
the hero of Campania whom the people forced to resign,
even as the pain and destruction were in full force.

Okay, the one-eyed shepherd is Hannibal, and the hero
of the battle at Campania is Claudius Marcellus,
who had to step down as consul (I forget exactly why).
Byrsian fire therefore is that inflicted by Carthage.

And look at us now! A barbarian in no way praiseworthy comes
to claim the woods, the sheep, the herds, and that noble wreath
which used to be so prized and honored among us all.

ARCHAS:
I think there you are wrong. This is what Latium wanted.

BATRACOS:
I have to admit it. The slightest threat of pain will cause
cowards to grant whatever is asked of them and even
appear enthusiastic. But if our forebears had seen
what we are doing now and what we have come to,
the gallant man of Mars would not have thrown himself
into the Stygian shadows. To sacrifice himself
to preserve us all for this ignominious moment?

The reference here is to Mettius Curtius, the famous
Roman who rode into the chasm that had opened
in the earth in the Forum, to placate the angry underworld gods.

The fathers would not have cast the souls of the brave below
doing battle against the prowling Senonian panther,
and the geese would have honked in vain to warn the young men of danger.
Parent and child would not have sacrificed each other
or had their entrails thrown to the Latin dogs to tear.

Senonian is the Latin adjective for Sens,
so this refers to a fight in Gaul. The geese cackled
and thereby saved Rome from surprise attack. The parent
and child are Decius and Publius Mus, who died
as described—but none of this will appear on any exam.

But why should I rehearse these well-known stories of those
holy labors and all the noble blood that was spilled

into the Rhine? Look, Mother, how Ercinia now
wins, alas, those titles and drags through the briars and mud
our grandchildren who yield their stars to the Cimbrian thugs.

Ercinia is code for Germany, and the other,
Cimbria, designates in a general way the north.

ARCHAS:
Dear Batracos, why renew these ancient complaints? Remember
the weeping back when Dalmatians, Pannonians, and Greeks
imposed their yokes upon our bulls—or worst of all
the Africans whom we had every reason to despise.
They drove your bulls across your fields for their own advantage
and profit. But what of it? They are all gone now.
I remember the sad taint of this upon my fields.

BATRACOS:
"My fields," you say? Tell me in what way are they yours.

ARCHAS:
You think of them as your own, as they've been for generations,
but do you forget that Amintas' offspring came here once,
and their great holdings extended to the farthest Indian mountains.
The waters of clear Eurotas and fair Aracinthus gave
laws to all of Maeonia once—until this was stolen
and at last came into your hands. You stole it; another
steals from you, which is how it goes, world without end.
Why is it such a great thing if Circius grabs these honors
or wears, at least for the moment, the laurel on his brow?

Amintas is Alexander. Much of Italy once
used to be Greek. "Naples" is nea-polis, said fast.

BATRACOS:

Egon was the greatest of the Latin shepherds, the one
to whom all men looked up with reverence and respect.
Daphnis was the second greatest, and he rose up
against the first and threw our fields into much confusion.
We had to choose between them, a difficult but needful
decision, and I went to Egon's side. He was
more just, I believed, and I'd been opposed to Daphnis
for complicated reasons. Circius is his successor,
and I worry lest he behave as Daphnis did, cutting down
our trees with axes and loosing wolves among our flocks.

Egon is the pope—that is, Clement VI.
Louis IV, of Bavaria, who became the Holy Roman
Emperor in 1328, is Daphnis.
He was succeeded by Charles IV (who is Circius here).
He was Count of Luxembourg and King of Bohemia too.

What refuge is there for me? Where can I flee? I fear
that the earth itself may open a chasm to swallow me up.
My mother has lost all sense of honor and decency
and for all I know may sell me to some vile brothel keeper.
With his laurel wreath on his head, Circius will be famous
and will lead the Furies from hell while crows crisscross in the air
sounding their raucous omens of evils that soon will come.

The mother, as I explained a short while ago, is Rome.

ARCHAS:

Have you lost all your strength so that you can no longer endure
their first attacks? Those men from the banks of the Rhine are soft,
their minds as well as their muscles grown flabby from easy living.
Fortify your sheepfolds as well as you can; dig ditches

around them and plant great thickets of brambles and thorns; let shepherds
put stakes in the ground to slow down any attackers. Call out
your Molossian hounds! Give every boy you have a slingshot.
Give especial care to paths of approach to the north.
It is often said that the gods will come to the aid of those
who've exerted themselves. The exertion can certainly do no harm.

BATRACOS:

All I have left are unwarlike, effeminate types. We too
have suffered from easy living, and now in a time of danger
what can we do? You see what a poor patch of land we have,
no seashore nearby, no broad inviting plain for maneuvers.
We have to go on foot through the hills and mountains to bring
food to our hungry flocks as well as our beasts of burden.

ARCHAS:

Get hold of yourself, woman. Banish doubt from your mind
and rouse your quavering heart. I have seen Amarillis
with tears streaming down her face. You suppose that she was glad
to bestow the crown on Circius' proud and eager head.
Not so. Nor was the woodland spangled with glad flowers.
No pipes played merry tunes; no trumpets blared forth. The Tiber
flowed in its bed in silence, as the solemn elders were silent.
Young athletes stood still, and the matrons' whisperings ceased. The mouth
of the sacred Lupercal cave stood shut. The games were wholly
lacking in any joy. Circius sat on his throne
and a wind from the south snatched off his laurel crown and swept it
northward. It flew in the air and there the leaves caught fire.
The people watched the sparks disappear in the near distance.

This description may be what Boccaccio wished had happened.
Contemporary accounts suggest that the coronation
of Charles was not unjoyful and that Romans cheered the procession.

Aruntes, whom the Arcadians hold in highest esteem,
reading the omen pronounced what he took to be its meaning:
"He'll make the journey northward and end his days near the Rhine.
In his tomb, his corpse will rot and the fame that he snatches here
will likewise disintegrate. Or else, if he should return,
for the smoke in the sky seemed to waver a bit toward the end,
whatever he has in mind, he will accomplish nothing."

BATRACOS:
O holy Pales, I pray you, confirm his interpretation
and make this omen good. See that the bicorn beast
returns to its lair in the north and no longer bothers our fields
with its pointed horns. We'll slaughter a nursing ewe in your honor.
And you, Archas, dear man, stay with me if you would,
for the night is coming on. Apollo departs and allows—
do you see them overhead?—the first stars to show themselves.

X 🐍 The Dark Valley

LYCIDAS:

Dorilus, poor fellow, it doesn't seem to matter
whether Orion sends rain to the earth, or Amon
flowers, or whether the Crab brings crickets to chirp in the heat,
or Chiron strips the leaves from the trees, I always see you
with your head bent and tears welling up from your sad eyes.
What is the source of this grief? Have all your grapevines died?

God knows who these people are. There are implausible guesses,
but it's easy to read as powerlessness and poverty (Dorilus)
and indifferent or wicked power ("Lycidas'" root is "wolf").
Orion, Amon (the Ram), the Crab, and the last one, Chiron
(Sagittarius), are the four seasons' constellations.

DORILUS:

With a fire bolt from the highest heaven that Jupiter flung,
the fields around us are flattened. He struck a mighty beech
that was famous in these woods. The earth groaned at the blow,
the leaves of the forest trembled, and birds took off in panic
to hide in nearby briars. Shepherds shut themselves
in their rustic huts and cowered, sure that the god was angry
at somebody's bad behavior, fraud, or some worse crime.

The tree is perhaps a leader. The late Thomas Bergen suggests
that this might be Prince Andrew, but that doesn't fit with the rest.
(I took one of his classes: he was a decent fellow,
but not altogether persuasive then or, it turns out, now.)

Contemptuous of our rustic freedoms, a wicked man
scattered the flocks and herds. His lusts went beyond all bounds
and even as Crisifabrus was preparing a sacrifice
to Juno for his marriage, he came and stole away
the bride from the wedding party—I mean the lovely Rufa.
And Phyllis, Phytias' girl, he also purloined. Remember
Ovid's account of the Centaurs and Lapiths and that feast
that turned into total carnage? These grotesque events
came a close second. I'll omit all the sordid details
except to say that he also took my sweetheart, and I
am bound with chains in a sunless cave where ivy and myrtle
never grow. This is why you see me weeping. But you?
In patches and covered in soot? A workman? What is your story?

"Crisifabrus" is something more or less akin
to "goldsmith." Nobody knows if the poet had in mind
a particular man. The sunless cave is a pastoral prison;
the ivy is very probably books of poems; and myrtle
is an attribute of Venus and its absence means loneliness.

LYCIDAS:
I see that Menalcas spoke the truth about this poor valley.
The sordid gifts of Plutarcus do not distress me so much
as the wicked deeds of a madman who's emerged somehow from the
    swamps
where bullfrogs live in the marshes and managed to come into power.

Plutarcus is the lord of the underworld—or Pluto.

DORILUS:

I hadn't recognized you. Forgive me. I took you for
Podarcis with the light behind you that way. These days
one cannot be too careful. But now my hopes revive.
You'll help restore blue skies, revive the fields and herds,
and freshen the valley's streams. I'll set up crowns of oak
behind the altars to thank both you and the heavenly gods.
Come into the cave with me. I cannot offer you much.
I have no milk or fruit or hazelnuts or wine.
Polipus took it all. Or nearly all. There is
some bread and water that I can share. I've made a bed
of ferns. I think I heard when I was a child that the gods
live on the earth this way when they condescend to visit.
Don't scorn it, then. At least you can wash your hands and face
with the water. You can rest your weary limbs for a while.
I'll put another log on the fire to warm us up.

LYCIDAS:

No, no. I'm sorry to say that you're wrong. What you see before you
isn't me, but a simulacrum. I'm not of this world,
not since Hermes' wand touched my head and robbed me
of light and air, and took a lock of my hair for Hecate.

DORILUS:

Poor fellow! I'm truly sorry. My hopes for safety are lost,
and I expect to die in this misery that now
darkens my days. Hylas drives the flock of sheep
to Micon's meadow to graze. His hands milk them. Another
fetches clover, leaves, and willow shoots to nourish
the lambs and the ewes. Yet another shears their heavy fleeces
and washes the wool in running streams. Another sings
or plays on the pipes he loves, while the boughs of the cypress sway
as if in time to his tune. Only I am alone,

fettered this way by Polipus, having committed no crime.
My hours, otherwise idle, are filled with lamentation.

LYCIDAS:

But answer me, I beg you, did the nine Castalian sisters
teach you to pass your days this way in endless weeping?
Your mind is in no way fettered! Your soul is always free!
Nothing keeps your imagination from wandering through
Sicilian pastures or Cretan woodlands. You can, if you choose,
climb Mount Ida's heights to converse with the shepherds there
or explore the peaks of Parnassus where the fragrant laurel grows.
Do not brood on injustice, but think what you have that no one
can take away. Have you never learned how to be content
without the world's poor trinkets or mankind's fickle opinion?
Argus gave us the laws of the gods of Mount Olympus;
blind Mopsus celebrated the Phrygian and the Danaan
shepherds; Tityrus had his farmlands taken away,
but that did not prevent him from singing of how, once, Turnus
had dyed them with blood. If tears are shed, they ought to be mine,
to whom nothing remains whatever. Do you remember
what I was in life, how great my holdings were,
the extent of my limitless powers? I have lost all but loss,
for nothing is left to me now but misery and ruin!

The Castalian spring on Parnassus is where the muses frolicked,
which explains that soubriquet. Hesiod is Argus;
blind Mopsus is Homer; Tityrus of course is Virgil,
Turnus being Aeneas' antagonist in his epic.

DORILUS:

Ah, Lycidas, I never thought to have so great
a consolation—and certainly not from you—for this
hard life of mine. But tell me, how do you get on

with Plutarcus? What is your existence like down there?
What are the valleys and plains that you have been wandering through
since Mercury deprived you of Apollo's blazing light?

LYCIDAS:
At the center of our world is Treneros, a cave
that the sun never sees. We are all led through its gaping mouth
where the huge black mastiff leaps and snarls, guarding the cavern,
nipping at the heels of any who move too slowly
and attacking those who would try to turn back and escape
without the prince's express permission. From there one can see
groves of trees, lakes, rivers . . . But all is dark
with fog and murk, and the beetling cliffs are black with soot.
We find ourselves in perpetual winter, perpetual night,
and we warm ourselves—but never enough—with invisible fires
that are not fed by fuel but the magic and will of the gods.
These are nothing at all like Sicily's pleasant pastures
or the meadows of Tyre, or the gardens of roses the Lebanese plant.
No flowers, no cheerful prospects of hillsides or curving beaches.
The rivers are not the beautiful Po but sluggish streams
that stink as they wind through barren fields of yew and crowsfoot.
Their banks are lined with a venomous slime. If there were beasts
or birds, they could not drink of such repellent foulness,
but vermin and snakes like it, and the scorpions from Egypt.
Here you sometimes pause to listen to nymphs that sing
sweet melodies in the woods or to sirens out on the rocks.
Down there are only bellows and screams—from lions or boars
or creatures even more fierce and beyond all imagination,
and the grim echoes repeat, resounding from those black cliffs.

DORILUS:
It sounds very bad. Could nature—or supernature—fashion
so vile a place, even there, deep in the bowels of the earth?

LYCIDAS:

Why ever not? The creator made the woods and the stars.
What could be beyond his capabilities? What
he can imagine, he can bring into being. But wait,
the worst is yet to come. Plutarcus sits on a huge
boulder next to his swarthy spouse in the blackest shadows
of the overhanging boughs and the canopy they affect
of a large sheepskin. Beside them, two of their courtiers stand:
Mange and Chill, who menace sheep and sorely afflict them,
bringing them fevers and death. Close by, a savage shepherd
covered with clinging serpents that wind about his limbs
plays on his instrument, but not the pipes or the lyre
that soothe and charm. Instead, he blasts on a long horn
that panics the flocks and rouses up the dreadful Furies
to run among the briars and stampede the maddened bulls
that run through those barren places destroying whatever they pass.
Count the stars in the sky or the grains of sand on the beach,
but the number of groans and cries one hears down there is greater.
From time to time, the mighty Jove hurls down his bolts
that shake the ground beneath us and illuminate for an instant
in ghastly glare our wretched state that the gloom has concealed.
The clouds pour down an icy rain mixed in with hail
while the winds howl and the wretched oak trees bend and break.
Those myriad souls that before were merely grieving now
flee in terror through thorns that tear them as they hurtle
about in every direction. Some of them come to a cliff
where they leap in desperation (but the dead cannot die again).
Then Diomedes' horses that feast on human flesh
come bearing down upon us, and Geryon's fierce hounds
bark and bite at random. We are driven on by hydras.
Demons on every side laugh in derision and fling
filth at us as herds of wild bulls charge and trample
and nests of vipers arise to writhe and torment us further.

There are stakes in the ground with their points sharpened in fires to
     wound
our already wretched and bleeding bodies. Packs of great wolves
descend from the hills howling to harry and do us hurt.
The worst that you can imagine comes nowhere close to the truth.

DORILUS:
Stop, stop! I beg you. I cannot bear to hear more.
What crimes could you have committed to deserve so dreadful a sentence?

LYCIDAS:
I think of them all the time now. For my theft of Micon's sheep
my punishment might suffice. But I seduced young boys,
ruining not only my own life but also theirs
in the woods' shadowy places—and for that I have to pay.

DORILUS:
It is said that Hercules dragged the fearsome three-jawed monster
out of those depths and rescued Theseus, Athens' king.
Do you want me to pray to Pan that you might be removed
to some milder and better place and released from that dark valley?

Those were, indeed, Hercules' feats but they suggest
how Christ harrowed hell. Pan, the woodland god
would also be a stand-in for the Christian deity.

LYCIDAS:
I am afraid my case is beyond the powers of prayer,
even yours, and Olympus is hardly likely to listen.
My torments are not much different than many of those whom the gods
have dispatched to the netherworld—for all I know, forever.
But let me tell you more of the demons who punish us all.
One drags hogs to a cliff and with his great strength dashes
them down to the rocks below where their limbs twitch and are still.

Another leads a pack of hounds from the heights of a mountain
until they are limp with fatigue and also tortured by plague,
at which time he lets them drink the water of stagnant marshes.
One drives bears from their caves and forces them into the sea
to swim as long as they can and watches them founder and drown,
or he swims out to be among them and with a huge iron hook
goes fishing for bears. Another casts evil spells on the lynxes
so that they can no longer eat and he studies how they starve.
I could go on even further, but it only gets grimmer and grimmer.
We live against our will and pray every day for a death
that never comes. But the sky is less dark in the east
and I must be gone, for I am forbidden Apollo's sight.
But I say to you do not despair. There is always hope.
Polipus may climb an oak tree, reach for a bird,
and fall and break his neck. And we will have one more guest
to swell our chorus of groans and our cries of exquisite pain.
The sisters spin out their threads, and nobody's runs forever.
Your fields will be yours again, while your chains will be taken from you.

DORILUS:
O Pan, whom we have honored here in these woodlands, grant
that what he says may happen. Come to us with your aid,
and we shall give thanks to you with our finest and fattest lamb
that we'll offer upon your altar. And we'll pray and play the games
that my songs of gratitude shall extend well into the evening.

XI § Pantheon

AUTHOR:

You follow Phoebus, pursuing the light—by which we mean
knowledge, of course—and it is your nature, Clio, to seek this,
for you are history's Muse, the first of the nine equals.
And what is history but knowledge collected through time?
For sentimental reasons, Apollo is fond of the laurel
and its leaves make up the crown of achievement that poets and scholars
forever strive to earn. Sit with me for a while
in the shade of these tall trees and help me as I sing
my songs for the great Mopsus. Bless my clumsy fingers
as I do my best to strum my Arethusan lyre.

For the poet to intrude in propria persona
into his poem is odd. But he can dress up as a shepherd
as well as anyone else. Think of one of those paintings
where the artist puts a likeness of his own face in the crowd.
Mopsus is still Petrarch, whom these poems were written to please.
Clio is, indeed, the muse. (In Virgil's Eclogue
VI, he begins by invoking her comic sister Thalia.)

In some secluded spot on top of a cliff good Glaucus
and his friend Amintas were building a little rustic fence
to protect the Berecinthian goddess whom they revered.

Boccaccio gives us the key, without which the cleverest reader
could never hope to guess who all these people could be.
Glaucus is St. Peter (they both were fishermen, right?)
and Amintas is St. Paul. The Berecinthian goddess
is Cybele (who in turn is a stand-in for the Virgin
Mary). Mount Berecinthus is a place where she was worshipped.

They accompanied their labors with a series of gentle murmurs,
and fair Mirtilis came, driving her heifers and goats
across the meadows along the banks of the River Tiber
and with the gentlest voice she ventured to address them:

Boccaccio also tells us that by Mirtilis he means
the Catholic Church—the leaves of the myrtle being
green on the upper side and blood-red on the bottom.
The red is for all the persecutions of early Christians;
the green represents their faith in the heavenly mercy of Christ.

"Father Glaucus, I see you twisting the willow branches
into much sturdier cords to string your fences. Prosper
and thrive, you and Amintas, and as you preside in these caves,
I beg you to take these bulls and goats of mine and tend them.
The bulls are healthy and paw the sand with impatient hoofs,
and the goats are rich in milk. Treat them kindly and give them
pastureland, water to drink, and now and again a song."

GLAUCUS:
Mirtilis, my dearly beloved, no clover is here.
I carry up from the valleys some grass to feed my modest
flock of lambs. I try to bear in the best of spirits
the scorn that those in Mount Rhodope's ancient forests show me,
as all the Arcadians do. And I do my best to avoid
the wicked Cacus, who steals whatever beasts he sees.

Cacus is the thief whom Hercules destroys—
it's in Virgil's Aeneid. *This makes Cacus the devil,*
or there could be an allusion to the King of France, who has stolen
the popes from Rome. It's possible, too, that Rhodope
is a play on the Rhodanus, the River Rhone, which flows
through Avignon, which is the chateau neuf des papes.

MIRTILIS:

I take your words as refusal, but I urge you to reconsider
and think of Hercules who, if you will remember,
slew the wicked Cacus. You cannot have quite forgotten
how he came to you once while you, in a small boat on the Jordan,
were out looking for fish. He put his hand on your head,
drew you to him, and placed his beloved flock in your care.
Do you suppose that his many all-but-impossible labors
were performed for you alone? He wished to help all creatures.

You will, I should imagine, have figured it out by this time—
that Hercules has been conflated here with Christ,
which has a certain neatness. The labors and the Passion
both result, after all, in splendid apotheoses.

I urge you then to have faith and to persevere. Your fields
are meager now and your flocks are pathetically few in number,
but your prospects are great and your meadowlands will surely prosper
with ever larger numbers of sheep and goats and cattle
than Amphion saw on the rich hillsides of Mount Aricanthus
or Apollo tended when he was employed as Admetos' shepherd.
Your assent to my request will not go unrewarded,
for I shall crown you with myrtle beneath the Tarpeian rock
and you shall dwell forever in my most loving embrace.
Lead the animals. Sing with your pipes to fill their ears
that strain to hear, and make the entire meadow resound.

GLAUCUS:
Mirtilis, you have won me over. I'll do as you ask
or, anyway, do my best. Prepare the pipes, Amintas,
and let the verses ascend as high as our ambitions.

AUTHOR:
And then, reaching down to the freshets of pious emotion that lay
in the depths of his heart, he commenced to sing his song of Jove
and his holy son, and the winds that sweep down through the valleys.
He explained to the grateful forest how God could be tripartite.
He sang of our first beginnings, the creation of land and sea
and sky in which stars shine and then in its turn the sun.

It doesn't at all diminish the fervor here to point out
that Boccaccio expects his readers to recognize
that this is a skillful reprise of Virgil's Eclogue VI,
the one in which Silenus performs in a similar way.
It's a nervy gesture inviting comparison to the work
of the greatest poet of Rome. It's a high standard to meet.

He explained the complications of how the rivers find
valleys in which to flow, and oceans and lakes have shorelines.
How do flowers wind up in places where they can grow?
How do great trees assemble into groves and expansive forests?
Where did the animals come from, and the birds that swoop and bank
in the sky above us? (And how did they first learn the art of flying?)
Who put fish in the sea and reptiles in hidden burrows?
Why are men unique in having minds and souls
and fates, for that matter, because in limited ways we remember
what happened yesterday and are able to predict
at least a little of what may occur today and tomorrow.
And who was the first man to figure out how to plant
seeds in the earth in springtime for the prospect of autumn harvests?
On the other hand, who first committed the terrible evil

of shedding innocent blood? Who was the herdsman who thought
to tame the cattle and sheep and send them into the meadow?
If you think of commonplace things, many turn out to be marvels.
Consider the brave and shrewd man who first subjected
metal to hot fire to be able to fashion tools.
Or take the reed pipe that shepherds learn to play
to produce intricate tunes. Who discovered that reeds
of different lengths will produce correspondingly different notes?
    In another and darker mode, he sang of Lycaon's crime
and Jupiter's great anger so that he inflicted a flood
that drowned all the beasts of the forest and domestic livestock as well.
We know what happened then, but still he sang about how
the pious Deucalion set forth in a boat with the seeds of things,
and his sons and their wives to provide the world with a second chance,
throwing rocks as they did and watching them turn into men.

You can read Deucalion's story in the Metamorphoses,
but clearly it's also Noah whom Boccaccio has in mind.

He sang of the giants' madness, who piled up enormous mountains,
putting Pelion on Ossa to make a mighty tower.

This too is a conflation of the story of those giants
who tried to assault heaven and also the Tower of Babel,
the Christianizing either being a way to tame
all those pagan myths, or perhaps to vouch for their truth.

He recounted the punishment that the heavens had meted out,
and how the flocks and herds bleated and lowed in confusion,
until the arrival of Archipater, who first observed
Silvanus' sacred rite that no one had seen before.

Archipater? The old father, or Abraham,
and Silvanus, who is the god of the forest, is Jehovah.

He sang of how Archipater left his ancestral fields
and the promises God made him and his aged and barren
wife, who laughed but nevertheless gave birth to a son.
At heaven's command the man was ready to sacrifice
that son, his own dear son, on a mountaintop on an altar.

The pretense of pastoral is no more than notional here:
we discern Abraham's story and Sarah's, and we remember
that the son she bore was Isaac, whose name in Hebrew is "laughter."

He rehearsed the sorry tale of the goats' deserved bereavement
and how the fire fell from heaven to scorch the woodlands;
how Cynaras got drunk and lay with his two daughters;
and then how someone sired the famous twins who fought.

Cynaras, unawares, had sex with his daughter, Myrrha,
so he stands in for Lot. Think of this all as a riff,
in which the question we have in the backs of our minds is how long
he can keep this up, and how neat each equation can be.

His performance then touched on the hungry boar and how
a blind old man was tricked when Sophronis made a goat
feel shaggy to the touch and therefore pass as a lamb.

This is Esau and Jacob, but why did he pick "Sophronis"
as a guise for Rebecca? In Greek it means "self-controlled"
or "guided by wisdom." Okay? Your assignment: figure it out.

The exile, the pastured flocks, the return, and then the vision
of a ladder up to the stars, and the dream that Stilbon had
of a strenuous wrestling match that went on all night long,
after which he was given—or had earned—another name.

Stilbon is one of the names for Mercury and therefore
apropos for heavenly messengers or angels,
or by extension even those who wrestle with angels.

Then, the shepherds' fraud, the boy sold into Egypt,
and his success there, helping Pharaoh interpret his vision.

Pharaoh, it seems to me, is cheating, but I am merely
translating. I can't step in to change things as I'd like.

Argus then is put in charge of the rich Pelusian harvests,
and he stores up grain that sooner or later draws his hungry
erstwhile friends to come south seeking aid in Memphis.

Pelusium is an Egyptian city up on the Nile
Delta not very far from Port Said. And Argus?
That's the name that he and Petrarch both have used
to indicate King Roberto. And Joseph, too, was "wise."

Then Foroneus snagged from a basket afloat in the river,
and the plagues that afflicted the Nile, and the poor goats drowned
        in the sea.

Foroneus, a mythical Argive, gave laws to his people.
Thus, Moses. Try not to smile at the goats in the sea.

The wandering in the desert, the water bubbling up
out of a rock, the bread that fell from the sky, the commands
of Jove, inscribed on stone on the peak of Idumea.

There is such a mountain, or range, and not too far from Sinai.

Osiris' idol, the tablets smashed, and the bites of the serpent
healed . . . He sang of all this, and then how the packs of dogs

were driven out of the fields with spears and bows, and the farmlands
won in the fierce battle meted out by the drawing of lots.
And the victory games! The races, the wrestling matches, and all
the celebration that one would expect on a festive occasion
at the splendid temple that they had erected of whitest marble . . .
But then were the herds and flocks stricken with dire diseases
and the soil was watered with blood. Lush forests were stripped
for wood for funeral pyres, and shepherds were taken away
to the banks of the Tigris to mourn and yearn to return home.
All this was accomplished because heavenly gods had willed it,
and although the prophets dreamt the causes and the corrections,
nobody heard their voices as they harrangued in vain.

GLAUCUS:
[There's a stage direction here Boccaccio puts in the text,
but that ought to be in brackets. Glaucus pauses a bit
to summon up the strength to continue with his song.]
Oh, I pray to heaven that they may allow me to sing
of even greater things. You Roman nymphs, help me!

AUTHOR:
He took up then how Maia's son descended from heaven
to announce to Diana the news of the holy word made flesh
in a virgin's womb, her honor remaining immaculate.

Maia's son is Mercury, messenger of the gods,
which corresponds more or less with Gabriel's role. Diana
is the pagan virgin goddess, conveniently at hand.

He prayed that men may have faith in the miracle, and the satyrs
began to dance and sing, and the nymphs and girls together,
all decked out in wreaths of various flowers and wearing
cinnabar makeup, joined in the celebration with cymbals
and the twangling strings of harps and lyres their fingers plucked.

The sun shone down with a special brightness on multicolored
flowers that filled the air with a mixture of sweet perfumes.
Phoebe's moon aligned with her brother's sun to produce
a new month, a new era. From the poles that glistened with dew
Jupiter poured fresh rain down to the thirsty meadows
in which kids leapt, birds twittered among the trees, and mountains
spewed forth festive fire. Then from the worthless bramble
olive trees began to sprout and grow. Ivy,
cedars, laurel, and palms revived to grace the shores
of the Adriatic, while grapevines appeared in their orderly rows,
bringing forth their precious jade and garnet fruit.
In the marshes those weeds grew that the shepherds make into baskets
while from above the willows offered their tender branches.
But why go on? It's enough to say that all things rejoiced
and competed in their gladness. Only Plutarcus wept
in his dark cave, more wretched than he'd ever been before.
He fortified his domain with iron gates and bars
to keep the wounded Codrus from managing to enter,
and he ordered the cruel sisters to keep a vigilant watch.

Plutarcus here is Satan, the lord of the underworld.
And Codrus? An Athenian king who gave his life
to save the city. His is the first of the seven different
names the poet uses when he wants to refer to Jesus.

Glaucus felt at the moment that he was celebrating
the joy that all creation was feeling, and its music
poured from his breast and chest, a threnody of praise.
He sang how the three shepherds came with gifts for the child,
following the star that led them across steep mountains
and wide deserts straight to the stable and the manger.
He told of the trip to Egypt with the infant snug in the lap
of the virgin mother—in flight from the ravening wolf, and the grief
for the lambs unjustly slaughtered. Then he sang of the youth

propounding the laws of Lycurgus and recounting the deeds of the ancients.
He told how Nathan washed in a stream to demonstrate
how by such immersion pigs could be cleansed of their filth.

Nathan, the Hebrew prophet who anointed Solomon, stands
here for John the Baptist. He's no mythological figure
but at least he is wearing a costume, which is what the party requires.

Water turned into wine; the bankers driven away;
the dead brought back to life by the art of this young man.
He sang how Pales produced acorns no oak had dropped,
and pious Actaeon gave his last commands at a supper
and how Menalcas betrayed him after the prayers were done.

Pales is that woodland deity who can be
of either gender. Actaeon, turned into a stag, was killed
by his own dogs, as Jesus was by his own people.
Menalcas is Judas, perhaps because the one in Virgil's
Eclogue III is described as wicked and malicious.

He sang how that man suffered innumerable bites
and then became Death's trophy, at which time rocks were split
and mountains shook as the earth trembled in spasms of anguish.
In daytime darkness spread through the air while sheep and cattle
bleated and bawled in the fear their herdsmen also felt.
Their ancestors rose up from their graves and tombs to roam
the forest again. He sang the labors of Hercules,
who broke through the rocks that barred the door of Cacus' cave
and retrieved the stolen herds of cows from that wicked man.
He sang how, after three days, Hippolytus' gashed limbs
rose up alive and how he appeared to the herds in the forest
in robes of triumph and decked with laurel wreaths and palms.
What a wonder it was to see what Jove was able to do!
Then, by his own motion, Phoebus arose to the stars

and poured bright rays of light on the friends he had left behind,
crowning them now as he himself had been crowned before.
These men dispersed to the north, the south, the east, and the west
to bring the word to the Britons and as far off as the Ganges.

This is all clear enough—the harrowing of hell,
the resurrection, and then the apostles' spreading the faith.
Asclepius revived Hippolytus from death,
and Phoebus Apollo ascends to the heavens every morning.

GLAUCUS:
O beautiful nymph, how many crimson blossoms, how many
white and yellow lilies will you see rising up
as you make your way along through the many lands and climes.
How many sacred temples will you pass from which the prayers
and offerings will come, given for Codrus' sake.
And he shall return when the earth melts in another fire
to divide the sheep from the goats at the end of days when plowboys
at last may rest. And there our song comes to an end.

AUTHOR:
While Glaucus sang, the Tiber's flow was hushed. Mirtilis
saw her bulls, when Glaucus had fallen silent, plunge
at once into the river to cleanse themselves of dirt
and, born again, mingle with Glaucus' herds and flocks
throughout the pasture, having heard his remarkable song.
Hesperus hung in the sky, reluctant to descend
into the sea as shadows climbed the mountainsides.
But it's time to go home now, lads. Summon your goats from the pasture.
I'll bind the laurel wreaths as the hills applaud the poet.

XII 🜂 Saphos

CALLIOPE:

What do you think you're doing, you impudent young man?
You stroll among these laurels plucking from this one or that
whatever you want or think you need. This grove is sacred!
Trespassers are not welcome, nor vandals, without the express
invitation of Juno—in recognition of merit.

ARISTAEUS:

Is my offense so great? I've picked a few of the smallest
leaves I could find, just two or three. I was drawn by the sweet
scent I could not resist. If you are the nymph or goddess
who rules this place, I invite you to come to my grove and shake
my oaks. You may take in exchange, whatever acorns fall.

*Calliope is the muse, the ninth of them, whose domain
is poetry. Aristaeus is Boccaccio's alter ego,
whom the poet describes in a letter as having been afflicted
by a stammer he managed in adolescence to overcome
and even achieve an eloquence everyone admired.
This may be an allusion to Boccaccio's change from mere
Italian to the Latin in which he is writing here.
The title is a tribute to Sappho, the poet of Lesbos.*

CALLIOPE:

You're kidding, right? There were, I think, some ancient cults
in which the oak was sacred to Jupiter. But now?
You compare your oaks to laurels? Acorns are fed to pigs,
while laurel leaves are for poets, whom Apollo recognizes
and welcomes to his grove and the fountain where the Muses
run their plectra over the strings of their lyres and sing.

ARISTAEUS:

Good lord! Apollo's grove? O lovely maiden, this
is what I was looking for, although I had no idea
that I had stumbled upon it serendipitously.
Where may I see that lady praised by Mopsus' verses
as well as by a flock of other poets and nymphs?

CALLIOPE:

Why do you want to do this? What is it that you want,
poking about in the shadows here in my sacred grove?

ARISTAEUS:

It's Saphos I'm looking for. Do you know her? Does she spend
the day at play in the grasses in some secluded dell?

CALLIOPE:

What business can a swineherd like you have with Saphos?

ARISTAEUS:

Why else would any young man want to meet great Saphos?
I burn with desire for her embrace. I left the crowds
behind me to try to find that woman who hasn't been seen.

CALLIOPE:

You? You want to embrace . . . her? Surely, you jest.
Perhaps your pigs would like to be kissed by the twinkling stars.

Foxes will fly, and the crane and the duck in harness will draw
enormous war chariots across the countryside.
Your job was cleaning out pigsties. You also treated dogs
afflicted by mange. Your hands are covered with briar scratches
and scarred by the bites of your hounds. You try to treat yourself
with ointments and elixirs, breathe smoke from galbanum resin,
or apply soft lumps of coal. You purge yourself with hellebore
to rid yourself of your sluggish guts' distressing wastes.
You roll in the grass with your pigs. And you want to court Saphos?
Why would you settle for her? How about Pallas Athena?

ARISTAEUS:
You must be thinking of some other fellow. Your crude description
has nothing whatever to do with me. Galathea loved me
and the beautiful Phyllis as well. Therefore why not Saphos?

*Galathea appears in Boccaccio's first eclogue
as "lovely Galla," so she could be merely some peasant girl
the poet had in mind. On the other hand, the name
is one that Petrarch uses to refer to his dear Laura.
Take your pick. And Phyllis? Another peasant name,
it could refer to the fans his Italian work had attracted.*

Now soft down is showing upon my cheeks, and Pan
has taught me the use of his pipes. I have learned new songs.
More to the point you should know that I come from excellent stock.
My mother was Cyrene, a Thessalian nymph. My name
is Aristaeus. I gather acorns and sweet honey
from the pleasant groves of my ancient Arcadian forest home.
I should have thought you would know to whom you have been speaking.

*An Aristaeus was an Acadian ruler who first
discovered the uses of honey and the secrets of apiculture.*

His mother was Cyrene, raped by Phoebus Apollo.
Her father was Peneus, god of the river of that name.

CALLIOPE:

Ah, yes, I place you now. I ought to have known. You are
like Critis, the judge from Ida. I saw you a while ago
singing some popular tune down at the village crossroads
with the rabble stamping their feet and applauding your performance.

Critis, of course, is a critic or judge. But the reference to Ida
compares him to Paris, who chose Aphrodite over the others,
which is to say he prefers love songs to more serious verse.

ARISTAEUS:

I admit it. That was me. But that was some time ago.
A man's intentions can change and his tastes. When I was younger
vulgar songs were pleasing enough, but all those pieces
I now disclaim. I gave them to Lemnos' crippled god.
Age has brought with it vision and longing for better things.

Lemnos' god is Vulcan, which is to say the fire.
Boccaccio did indeed burn some of his early work.

CALLIOPE:

Good heavens! Only recently this unprepossessing busker
could barely carry a tune. And now he intends to climb
to the summit of Mount Parnassus. Because he is in love!
The gods can do what they like, having such awesome powers,
but are they sentimental and attracted by mere need?

ARISTAEUS:

I'm glad you find me amusing. But tell me, lovely nymph,
where are my maiden's caves? I am burning up with ardor.

CALLIOPE:

Are you sure that your great desire isn't still for Phyllis?
Or Lupica, whom you can lure with a small basket of apples?
The goddess you say you want is difficult to approach,
and very few can rightly claim to be her suitors.

ARISTAEUS:

That Lydian shepherd once beheld the wife of Mars
and two other goddesses with her, absolutely naked
under the tall oak trees. Why can't I see Saphos?

It's the judgment of Paris. The wife of Mars is Aphrodite.
And the other two? Correct! Hera and Athena.

CALLIOPE:

That's what the goddesses wanted. But how do you know Saphos?

ARISTAEUS:

Silvanus met Minciades yesterday where the Sorge
River arises to wind its way through sleepy Vaucluse.
In the shade of an ancient holm oak, they sat together and talked.

Silvanus is the pastoral name that Petrarch takes
for himself; Minciades is Virgil (from the name of Mantua's river).
The Vaucluse is a part of Provence where Petrarch lived for a time.

They had shaded their eyes with oak's green leaves and they were singing
in rival songs, their excellent voices ascending to heaven.
They had left the care of the pigs and slopping the swill to Gaetha.
Both with their pipes and their voices, these men gave praise to Saphos
that echoed through the valley. Delighted by this and amazed,
I forgot at that instant Phyllis as I felt a new tremor possess me,
and with their music in mind I search for her now and I long

to visit those caves in which she dwells. I have never seen her,
but there is such a thing as love before first sight.
You are not she, I take it? Your face and your speech and gestures
lead me to infer that you are no mere mortal.

CALLIOPE:

I am not Saphos but merely one of her servants. Still,
I can tell you that the path you have chosen won't be easy.
It's a shameful thing to admit that you've aimed too high, but pride
may not be enough to sustain you. It will be an enormous labor.

ARISTAEUS:

What is Saphos like then? More beautiful than you?
You far outshine my woodland Phyllis or fair Delia.
Tell me your name and let me know from whom you descend.
It could well be that I've somehow heard of you, fair maiden.

CALLIOPE:

You may have, for I am Calliope, daughter of mighty Jove
and guardian of the Castalian grove and the famous fountain.
But within your wood there are only a few who have heard of me.

ARISTAEUS:

No, no. I have heard old Minciades singing your praises,
and Silvanus, in his cave, referred to you with reverence.
You teach the forest its music, the birds how to sing, the dumb
rocks to resound. It is your voice that inspired Saphos
to produce those elegant poems she draws from her heart and mind.
But tell me, if you would, where lovely Saphos dwells.

CALLIOPE:

Pan's dearest daughter, Saphos, stays on Nysa's heights,
where she makes her home beside the sweet gorgonian spring.

This is a complicated name for the Hippocrene,
which was formed when Pegasus' hoof struck the ground. You remember
that Pegasus sprang from the blood of Medusa—one of the gorgons.
You can make the connection and then congratulate yourself.
Pan invented the musical pipes. Boccaccio elsewhere
calls him the universal body of nature. Nysa
is the other—and less well known—peak of Mount Parnassus.

The sight of her starry eyes and beatific visage
has rarely been allowed to peasants like you. Laurel
wreathes her head and veils her incredibly beautiful face.
My sister Muses and I all wait on her and attend her,
and to her from time to time the god Apollo sings.

ARISTAEUS:
Why does she live on top of a mountain? Why reject
the lively life of cities? Why is she so reclusive,
hiding herself away so that nobody can see her?

CALLIOPE:
She likes her privacy in which she can meditate
on the forest's mysteries and wonders. Sitting still,
she can venture down to Plutarcus' blackened domain
and see the lamentation down there. She can contemplate
the secrets of the sea in those groves beneath the waves,
and lead the Phorcinides in their choruses of praise.
Or she can seek the Elysian hills and their fortunate meadows
with their tranquil flowers, their gently rustling green leaves,
their twittering birds, and overhead the spangle of stars.
And all these things that she sees in her mind's eye she transmutes
with the well-tuned strings of her lyre to profound and elegant songs
that she stores in an envelope of green morocco leather.
You think the rabble would let her do these things? The mobs
in the city squares have neither the taste nor even the patience

these delicate works demand. They shout as they herd their goats
making a never-ending distraction with what they suppose
is life. Calm and quiet is what my goddess seeks
and these she finds on that inaccessible mountaintop.
When the flowers Chiron hides come up at last in springtime,
we trample them underfoot, careless and inattentive.
From this she has retreated into her lofty cave
and hidden her chaste face behind the sacred laurel.

The Phorcinides are the daughters of Phorcis, a sea god.
Chiron is the centaur, a winter constellation.
(It's another one of Boccaccio's show-off carom shots.)

ARISTAEUS:
Once on Mount Aracinthus, I saw a famous shepherd
piping a heavenly song, but he came to a sad end
and was carried off by deadly hemlock. I also beheld
one of the bravest herdsmen destroying the Punic lions
that had come to plunder the sheepfolds of the peaceful Latin farmlands.
To have seen these things is a wonder for which I shall always be grateful.

Socrates is the famous shepherd. The brave herdsman
is Scipio Africanus. The point is that great wisdom
and virtue are neither recognized nor honored by mobs.

CALLIOPE:
When holiness descends into the workaday world
it loses its luster and people tend to take it for granted.
There are some who have had the nerve to slander this innocent lady
or deface her pious brow. So of course she turns away.

ARISTAEUS:
What possible slanders? What stains? Tell me more, I beg you!

CALLIOPE:
Many who fail to understand how to interpret
her words have called her a liar. They say she distracts young men
and leads them into frivolity and irresponsible conduct.
Some say that she is not to be trusted, being connected
as she often is with theater actors and mimes, who feign
and pretend and therefore blur the line between fiction and truth.
Some say she misinterprets history, confusing
our minds and our ideas of the noble deeds of our forebears.
Still others think she is only greedy for wealth and fame
and merely uses her art as a way to promote herself.
Annoyed by these kinds of insults, she keeps to herself on the mountain.

ARISTAEUS:
I can imagine drunken men at the sacrifice
of a pig to Demeter or maybe a goat to Bacchus, rowdy
and inclined to vulgar joking, blurting out these remarks.
But who would pay attention? Such calumnies fade in the air.

CALLIOPE:
No, it's the best men in the woods who say these things.

ARISTAEUS:
Who? How can intelligent men say stupid things?

CALLIOPE:
Don't pretend to be so surprised. It often happens.

ARISTAEUS:
You'll have to explain, I'm afraid. You're not talking now to Plato.
I'm just a simple shepherd and I do not understand.

CALLIOPE:

There are men who can save cattle the wolves have snatched away
and are famous for their elaborate speechifying. Others
claim to know the causes of various ailments afflicting
cows and sheep and tell us which are the healthy springs,
and boast that they can alter the fates and change the forest's
fortunes. These are proud and serious people who say
where the gods live and what they want and how to behave
to avoid their wrath. They know the expiatory rites
that can keep the thunderbolts of angry heaven from striking.

These not unentertaining descriptions apply to lawyers
and then to physicians you don't expect to find in the woods.

ARISTAEUS:

What would they know of the delicate art of singing? Farmers
drive their oxen through fields and cleave the earth with a plow,
while shepherds urge their sheep into pastures using a crook.
Neither has any idea how the other works and lives.
The vintner tends his vines that are growing in orderly rows,
and the cheese maker milks his sheep or goats or cows and produces
his smelly cheeses. None is aware of the others, and none
is content with his own life. This is why bulls and lions
hate each other. Contempt such as you describe is not
altogether surprising. But please, show me the way
by which I can climb Parnassus to behold Saphos singing.

CALLIOPE:

There is a path, but fallen branches and tangled briars
have all but obliterated many parts of it. Rocks
obstruct it here and there, and dust the wind has heaped
has obscured some of its twists and turns. There are greedy hunters
who have roamed the hillside and ruined some of the old approaches
which have not been tended for years, or, indeed, for centuries.

Many men have set out, hardy and resolute,
but the sight of the steep gulleys has made them turn back soon enough
to seek easier lives here in the lowland meadows.

ARISTAEUS:
I have already climbed Lycaeus' challenging cliffs
and am not an absolute novice. And I know what to expect.
It requires strength, of course, but also strength of will.

The Arcadian Mount Lycaeus is supposedly Pan's birthplace.

CALLIOPE:
How does one distinguish strength of will from intention
or mere desire? The obstacles I've spoken of are real.
In vain did Arpinas try, sweating and clambering upward,
and everyone supposed he had the strength and skill.

Arpinas is Cicero, who tried to write poems but couldn't.
His birthplace was Arpinum—but then you have to know that.

ARISTAEUS:
He did not have my passion. Or whatever one is born with.
The path may be hard and painful but not to venture upon it
is even worse and is full of bitterness and anguish.

CALLIOPE:
If you refuse to heed my words of warning and wish
to see the sacred fountain where Saphos lives, you must listen
to this advice which I relay from her. Each man
must somehow find his own way. We are forbidden to guide you,
except to suggest that you study those who have made the ascent.
Silvanus not long ago scaled the impossible peak,
but few, since Minciades' death, have managed to do so—
except for Opheltis, who sang of the slaughter of many sheep.

Start with him and learn whatever it is he can teach you,
what friends gave him aid, what paths of ascent he discovered,
and how he succeeded at last in reaching the difficult peak.

*Opheltis is Lucan, who wrote of the civil war between Caesar
and Pompey—in the* Pharsalia, *which Boccaccio admired.*

ARISTAEUS:
I guess I'll go and talk to Silvanus, who lives near by.
I'll bring a couple of piglets as gifts. It never hurts.

XIII ❧ The Laurel Wreath

DAPHNIS:

Stilbon, how good it is to see you here at leisure,
pausing between your strenuous enterprises. You climb
difficult Alpine passes and exert yourself to bring
the pricey gems that sometimes come to light in the current
of frigid rivers. But now you recline for a while in the shade.

Daphnis is any poet, for poets are honored with laurel,
which is what Daphne became. Stilbon is some merchant;
the name is one of those that Mercury uses, the patron
of merchants. Boccaccio had an argument like this
with an actual Genoese tradesman (no name has been supplied).

STILBON:

Beneath this towering cliff, Amilcas was tending
his goats, while the fair Phaselis was gathering willow branches
to weave them into the gaps of some of her damaged fences.
They kept the adult goats but they gave me some of the kids
to settle a debt. So here I am, at least for the moment.
But while I lie at ease, you are all hustle and bustle,
roaming through the valleys, a feverish *homme d'affaires*.

DAPHNIS:

It's true, but we do not get to choose. I'll refresh my goats
and chat with you until the heat of the day subsides.

STILBON:

Splendid idea. Let the goats drink from the little stream there,
while you and I pass the time in pleasant conversation.
Tell me, friend, what kinds of troubles furrow your brow.

DAPHNIS:

Oddly enough it's these gentle breezes that we can feel.
They remind me of my own Gargaphian valleys. I miss them
and I miss my dearest Elpis about whom I used to sing,
the very fairest of all the maidens who dwell in these woods.

Gargaphia is a spring sacred to Diana,
but that may only be a stand-in for some other place
near Naples. And the poet writes in his own hand
in the manuscript margin that "Elpis" is a Greek word meaning "hope."

STILBON:

I know an Elpis, but she may not be the one you mean.
She is a friend of Crisis. They cannot be the same.

Has the penny dropped? The merchant and poet have different Hopes.
The merchant's is a friend of "Crisis," or, bluntly, gold.

DAPHNIS:

The Elpis I know and love is the one whose companions are nymphs
that live on the peak of Nysa. I don't believe they're the same.

STILBON:

They say that love is blind, but what they mean is that we
are blind who follow it. One man adores the Muses,

even though that almost always means he'll be poor.
Still, of all the heavenly gods and goddesses, he
chooses them and follows Aphrodite's prompting.
He'll live on laurel berries and sleep on a bed of weeds,
and with a pale face recite his poems and dithryambs
dense with hidden meanings. Tityrus sang by the Tiber
of the Tyrian shepherds who struggled against the Argolian bulls,
but what good did that do him? He could not fill his belly
with the cool waters that flow from the Muses' lofty fountain.

Tityrus, of course, is Virgil. There's a character of that name
in his first eclogue (the Tiber is also a broad hint).
The shepherds and bulls are the Trojans and Italians in the Aeneid.

DAPHNIS:
You paint a dismal picture of a life that is not so bad.
We have on our tables olives, apples, and other fruit,
and our beds are strewn with leaves that rustle agreeably
as we shift our positions in sleep while Nursia plays her nocturnes.
What seems to be unpleasant is the king who turned the sand
beneath his feet to gold, or that crazy Parthian ruler
who drank molten gold. It isn't always a blessing.

The first is Midas, whose touch turned everything to gold.
The Parthian king is Crassus. His case is just as extreme.

We live immune from such greed and, content with little, fear
less than the wealthy do, for what have we got worth stealing?
The monster that afflicts so many men of business
pays us no mind. Our ornaments are laurel boughs and are free.

STILBON:
Such events as you mention are extremely rare. Think rather
of how many animals Taurus pastured for Amintas,

how many Pindus kept for your much-admired Mopsus,
Menalus for Argus, Eurotas for Polibus,
or Erimantus for Phorbantis. Their flocks were small.
On the other hand, count the animals and the servants
of Hercules, or the burial mounds of ancient Egypt.
You see what a difference there is. Money maketh a man!
Your foolish talk about how the Boeotian rocks have flown,
or the rivers turned back in their courses, or oaks uprooting themselves
in order to dance when some Muse strummed a chord on her lyre . . .
It's unpersuasive nonsense. And who needs dancing trees?

Amintas, Mopsus, Argus, Polibus, and Phorbantis
are poets; the other names are the regions that they come from.

DAPHNIS:
On the other hand, you have to admit that Crisis is fickle,
and can, for little reason or none at all, reject
a suitor to whom she has shown her favors before, breaking
their hearts with this change in fortune. But let us keep our discussion
free of any rancor. Let us contest in song.
You are Ligurian; I am a Tuscan. Here we are met,
and you have your pipes, I see, conveniently strapped to your neck,
while I have my reed pipe. Both of us are prepared.

STILBON:
You think I'd try to evade the challenge you offer? No, sir,
I'm ready and eager. You may have had your Arcadian teachers,
but I have these pipes that Hermes invented and gave to me.
Let's wager on it—a calf would be an appropriate prize,
the fattest one in the herd, with its mother bawling in grief.

DAPHNIS:
My flock, as you see, is tiny. I don't have a calf. A goat?
I'm afraid that that's the very best I can do, if you will accept it.

STILBON:

Done! I accept the terms. I expect, after all, to win.
My skill is rather better than I think you think it is.
But who will serve as the judge in this competition between us?

DAPHNIS:

Look down there a little. It's Critis, isn't it, washing
fleeces in the water and combing out the burrs?
Critis! I say, come here! Can you do us a small favor
and judge between our verses? You are a neutral party,
a friend to both but not too good a friend to either.
We have a difficult task, and the stakes are by no means small.

CRITIS:

Sure, I've got to wait until this sheep is dry,
and it will be good to be diverted this way. The stream
murmurs softly; the birds are not at the moment distracting.
Why not? Stilbon, you can go first and afterward Daphnis
can respond however he likes. Whenever you both are ready . . .

STILBON:

I shall offer my precious pipes to the sacred oak
if I should acquit myself well enough to win.

DAPHNIS:

And I make a similar promise of my reed pipes to the laurel.

STILBON:

My love is the generous Crisis, who makes my labors easy
and my life sweet. She marks out woodland paths for me
and writes down upon leaves the affection she has for me.
There are also instructions, sometimes, which I endeavor to follow.

DAPHNIS:

My love is Saphos from Lesbos, who bounds into my embrace
whenever I wander among the shadows of leafy groves.
With attention and care she inscribes my songs on slabs of marble
and she puts my name with those of the others she has favored.

STILBON:

On the island of Carpathos, Proteus keeps a thousand
calves for me, and on Corsica I have as many goats
and sheep that my man Dilos looks after and milks.
I also have donkeys there that Alipos raises and trains.

DAPHNIS:

In Arcadia on Mount Menalus' heights I have as many
heifers. Silvanus shows them the springs and brooks and meadows,
and at the base of Parnassus the singing of the Muses
makes the ewes grow wooly and bring forth many lambs.

STILBON:

Thalasson taught nobody but me to yoke the dolphins
and drive great whales with halters. I vanquished the trumpeting tritons
and managed to impose my will upon Phorcis' daughters.

This is a reach. The name comes from the Greek for "sea,"
and he means that trading vessels can be a source of profit.

DAPHNIS:

And Phoebus taught me how to limit Thalasson's powers
and even to overcome savage pythons. My reeds
can set the gods at one another's throats, while we brighten
the grove, and indeed the entire woodland, with our song.

STILBON:

A Massican plants and tends my fields. A Garganian guards
my flocks. And our Ligurian tends our delicate vines.
A Cretan holds the nets with which we harvest olives,
and a Hyblian cares for the bees. We even have a Briton
who looks after the herds. If I am in need of incense,
I have a Lebanese who sends me the best there is.

DAPHNIS:

Who created heaven and furnished it with stars?
Who decked the many trees in the forest with green leaves
and gave them seeds with which to reproduce themselves?
The fortunes of our people, both triumphs and defeats,
Pallas weaves for me with her great skill at the loom.

STILBON:

By what I do, the northernmost people learn to enjoy
coconuts and dates. Does Meroe have a taste
for lingonberry jelly from Sweden, or out on the Ebro
do they season their food with Indian spices that I provide?

DAPHNIS:

I have a voice stronger than iron and laurel that lasts
as long as time, and with this I tell the people of Spain
what India looks like and how they live there and what
they believe. I can even visit the underworld and report
to those in the upper air what the wraiths and shadows know.

STILBON:

Eleusis' vines will crown the sacred statues of Ceres,
and Cynthius will steal the flutes and drums of Bacchus,
or men will begin to sacrifice stinking goats to Venus
if ever Mopsus' pipes surpass the practical powers
of modest Amilcas—who cannot carry a tune.

DAPHNIS:

As long as ivy climbs the trunks of elms, as long
as laurel grows along the banks of rivers, as long
as myrtles spring up on the shore, even the lowly Bavus
will count in the end for more than Amilcas can imagine.

*Mopsus still means Petrarch. In a show of humility "lowly
Bavus" is the name Boccaccio takes for himself.*

STILBON:

The sailors will sing of the love of sea nymphs and the sirens
while all you poets molder in silence in unmarked graves.
Aeolus is our patron and Palaemon the great sea god
looks after us. Meanwhile the ungrateful Muses gather
at the lip of their fountain to laugh at the verses of mere mortals.

DAPHNIS:

We poets sing of heroes and valiant deeds. A rock
can undo all your sailors' plans and bring them to grief.
The Muses preserve our songs, but your wretches are brought down
to watery graves by the fickle Aeolus and Palaemon.

STILBON:

What water can do to us, fire can do to you,
and a few sparks on the wind can destroy a thousand scrolls
and set the Muses to singing dirges on their lutes.
You put your trust in papyrus, frailer than any ship.

DAPHNIS:

I think of how Amintas dispersed the Cilician pirates
so that they all disappeared to wherever their ships could take them.
Just so, a proud serpent will come to trample the necks
of Ligurian upstarts and scatter those ill-bred, shaggy goats.

This is the danger of pastoral doublespeak. Amintas
is almost certainly Pompey, who attacked a pirate stronghold
in Cilicia (which for a while was Armenian but now
is part of Turkey). The serpent? It's on the Visconti shield,
which makes this a prediction of the struggle between Milan
and the Genoese (Liguria). He's saying Milan will win.

CRITIS:
You both sounded fine to me. I say, call it a draw.
You win the cow and you win the goat. But enough's enough.
It's time for me to get busy and shear my wooly ewes.

XIV ❧ Olympia

SILVIUS:

It seems that the woods are full of birdsong as if the gods
were happy, and yet I see that Lycus is running around
whimpering and barking and wagging his stumpy tail
in excitement. What could it be? Is it good or bad? Go,
find out what's bothering him and bring me back a report.

CAMALUS:

That's Silvius for you. He has some kind of disturbing dream
and he wants us to go and look to see if it's true, while he
sprawls on his comfy couch. There's no rest for the weary.
The lives of servants are hard and never seem to improve.

SILVIUS:

When the stars rise in the west and deer attack the lions,
then servants will do their masters' bidding without complaining.
You don't like working for me? Go, find other employment.
Therapon, you go. Look in the stable. See
what is upsetting the dog. Then come and let me know.

Boccaccio makes it clear that Silvius means him.
He had the idea for this poem while walking one day in the woods.
"Camalos," he says, is Greek for "lazy," as servants

often are. And "Therapon" he admits is a word
the meaning of which he used to know but now has forgotten,
so he'd have to look it up. (What it means is "servant"
or maybe "helper." "Therapy" is derived from that Greek word.)

THERAPON:

Get up, old man! It's a fire! It's nighttime but you can see
the oaks around us. All the woods are burning up.
The flames are close to the house. I was terrified to see it
and ran back inside to warn you. Hurry! It's very bad!

SILVIUS:

O Pan, god of shepherds, be merciful to us. Help us!
You two, run and fetch water. But wait a minute. Hold on!
This is very peculiar. It's light, just as you say,
but there isn't flame or fire. Look how the trees are green
and the leaves are perfectly fresh in this eerie luminescence.
It's almost as bright as day but there doesn't seem to be heat.
Look at how those beech trees seem quite undisturbed.

THERAPON:

Overhead there are stars, which means that it is still nighttime,
but the woods are almost as bright as they are at midday. What
could it mean? Is this a portent of something about to happen?

SILVIUS:

Nature forgets herself. I've never seen it happen
that day and night are mingled together in this odd way.
There is no sun in the sky, nor moon, but we can see
as if there were. And the air is fragrant as if with flowers
everywhere in bloom, or spices as if we had been
instantly transported to fragrant Sabaean groves.
There even seems to be music echoing faintly. The gods
have come to earth? Or rather are we ascending to heaven?

OLYMPIA:

My dearest father! It's me, your daughter. Don't be afraid.
Don't turn your face away or try to rub doubt from your eyes.

Olympia is Boccaccio's daughter, Violante,
who died when she was five-and-a-half. The name he uses
for her, as he explains, is "heavenly, full of light."

SILVIUS:

Am I dreaming? Is this real? It is her face, her voice
that I have lost and now fear all the more to lose
again. If it is a fantasy, then I fear it may fade.
The minds of fond old fools like me are not to be trusted.
I'll ask whether the others are able to see this, too.

OLYMPIA:

Why do you doubt me, father? Do you think that I would come
to trick you? Or to trifle? I have the gods' permission
to come to pay you a visit and wipe away your tears.

SILVIUS:

My own dear girl! I believe! You are not merely a dream,
a projection of my love and grief. You were my hope,
my life. And to see you now, even if only briefly,
is the greatest gift the gods who took you from me could offer.
I was climbing the foothills of Vesuvius when I heard
from Fusca that you had been snatched away from us and now
were nestled in Cybele's lap. I was utterly wretched
and groaned and wept as I have been weeping ever since.

"Fusca" means dark, and is either the dark of mourning or else
an equivalent for Boccaccio's wife's real name, which was Bruna
di Ciango da Montemagno. The name means "having dark hair."
Cybele's lap is the earth, in a roundabout, hopeful way.

But tell me, dearest daughter, if I am worthy to hear,
in what woods have you roamed since you went away?
From whom did you get that impressive white robe stitched with gold?
What is this light we see that seems to come from your eyes?
Who are your companions? I can hardly believe how you've grown
in such a short time. You were only a little girl, but now
you seem to be ready for marriage. Tell me whatever you can.

OLYMPIA:

The garment you gave me is safe in Cybele's keeping. This
the virgin gave me as well as my beauty of face and form.
I've spent much time with her. But look at my companions!
You recognize them, don't you? You have seen them often before.

SILVIUS:

I have? My mind is a blank. I must admit, however,
that they are as fair as Narcissus, or Daphnis, or handsome Alexis.

OLYMPIA:

You don't recognize your sons? Marius and Iulus?
And my sisters? Have they changed so much? They are your own
precious departed children, my brothers and my sisters.

SILVIUS:

I had never seen those boyish cheeks covered with down.
Come to me! Let us hug each other and kiss. My soul
is full to overflowing of paternal love and joy.
O Pan and great Silvanus, what praises shall I sing
to thank you for this moment? Let us have wrestling matches
between you two as they did in ancient times, and the trophies
will hang high in the beech trees. Prepare the bowls of wine.
Sing the songs of Bacchus and deck the gods with garlands.
Raise up the altars to Hecate and fetch me a white ewe

and a black one for the goddess of Night. Bring pipes. Bring flowers.
Therapon, don't just stand there. Do, for once, what I ask!

OLYMPIA:
Silvius, calm yourself. We have our pipes and garlands.
If it is your desire to celebrate our arrival
we can sing tunes for you that these woods have never heard.

SILVIUS:
The woods are hushed in rapt anticipation. The Arno
suspends its whisper. The fields have fallen silent, waiting.
And you, you layabouts, will also please keep quiet.

OLYMPIA:
We enjoy eternal life, the gift of the great Codrus
through his divine power. Having descended from heaven
into a virgin's lap, he brought back the golden age.
He suffered the shepherds' shameful taunts and terrible insults,
was affixed to a cedar tree, and triumphed over death.
We enjoy eternal life, the gift of the great Codrus
through his divine power. The terrible old diseases
that infected the flock he washed away with his own blood.
Then he came down to Plutarcus' dismal and terrifying
valleys to break the pens and lead his father's flocks
and herds back up and into the light of brilliant sunshine.
We enjoy eternal life, the gift of the great Codrus
through his divine power. At last every single sheep
will dress itself again in the fleece it used to wear.
He'll separate the sheep from the goats. The latter he'll leave
for the predatory beasts, but the sheep will dwell in peace
in a gentle heaven in which there is no more time or decay.
We enjoy eternal life, the gift of the great Codrus.

SILVIUS:

Splendid! What fools we are to suppose that our local shepherds
can sing. I have heard of the feats of Orpheus, whose music
could move the stones and boulders, but I cannot concede that he
was better in any way than my daughter's performance just now.
What clarity, what timbres, what expressiveness there was!
Calliope herself could not have done any better,
nor the god who dwells in the Pythian cave where the oracles sit.
The oaks bent down their topmost leaves and the nymphs came out
as far as they dared to the very edge of the light to listen.
Savage wolves were hushed and the sheepdogs all fell silent.
But more than the impressive sweetness, there was the meaning,
inspiring and uplifting. Arcadian Mopsus never
addressed these amazing truths we have just heard, nor Tityrus.
This singing moves the soul. Let snowy doves be given
to all the girls and Ischirian bows to all the boys.

Mopsus here is Homer. Tityrus, then, is Virgil.

OLYMPIA:

You're very sweet, dear father. But we don't need any gifts.
Nothing mortal touches the land that we inhabit.
In eternity's realm the transitory disappears.

SILVIUS:

What is that realm like? What is the home that awaits
those of us who deserve it? Will the grass there give us sleep
and will crystal streams fill each of our goblets? The table
I have imagined is under the shade of the tall oak trees,
and there we will feast upon chestnuts, sweet ripe apples, and cheese
that the fertile flock will offer. Is it anything like that?

OLYMPIA:

Dear, sweet father! I told you that Cybele holds my shroud.
I am not the person I was when I departed.
I have joined with the gods who dwell on the peak of Mount Olympus,
to which my companions and I must now return. We bid you
the fondest farewell until we shall be reunited one day.

SILVIUS:

I shall die of grief if you leave me a second time, dear daughter.

OLYMPIA:

Do not weep, dear father. Tears cannot change fate.
All creatures in the woods were born and have to die.
I have already done what you will do one day.
Do not envy the gods for their immortality
but know that you as well will find after your death
the rest that awaits you. Rather give praises to heaven and thanks
on my behalf, for in dying I triumphed over death
and escaped the toils and sorrows that woodland life imposes.
We are parting for only a little while—and then we shall live
together through all of the endless years and infinite eons.

SILVIUS:

I hear you and I try to believe what you tell me, daughter,
but I am old and tears are welling up in my eyes.
To see you leave me again, a second time snatched from my arms . . .
But where, after death, shall I find you? In what meadow or glen?

OLYMPIA:

The Elysian fields I now return to. When you ascend,
that is where you will find me. It will not be difficult.

SILVIUS:

The Mantuan poet sang of Elysium, I remember,
on reeds he played with such skill that no one has ever been better.
Is Elysium as he describes it at all like yours?
Is this the abode of faithful spirits the gods have chosen?

OLYMPIA:

His vision was such that he could perceive great things, but he
could not imagine all of the beauties and wonders the spirits
enjoy in these sweet demesnes that are pleasing enough for gods.

SILVIUS:

What did he not see? Or perhaps leave out on purpose?
Among what mountain peaks is it set, or along what shores?
It may comfort my grief to hear you tell what to expect
and may rouse in me the desire to see this place for myself.

OLYMPIA:

Far off there is indeed a craggy mountain that no
sickly sheep can negotiate. The light of Phoebus
arises from below. Upon the peak in a forest
palm trees raise their slender trunks to the stars, and laurels
and groves of fragrant cedars as well as Pallas Athena's
beloved olive trees whose branches augur peace.
There is every kind of flower that you have ever seen
as well as some that you haven't offering up their perfumes
that are born on the gentle breezes. Who can describe the many
streams that flow like silver, winding their way through the grass
with a cheerful murmur as trees luxuriate on either
side, producing blossoms and then incredible fruit
compared to which the Hesperides' golden apples are mere
produce? Overhead, amazing golden birds
crisscross in the sky while bucks with golden horns
cavort upon the greensward as the gentle does look on

and lambs with snowy fleeces that are touched with gold by the sunlight.
There are heifers of course, and cows and bulls, all marked with gold,
and tame lions and even gryphons with great manes
that also seem to be gilded. We have your golden sun
and silver moon, but the stars are larger than any that you
have ever seen. It is always springtime there, and the heat
of summer never comes, nor the biting cold of winter.
There is neither fog nor even the dark of night. Discord
cannot be found, and death and weak old age are absent.
There are no cares, no wants, no pains, but only contentment.
To formulate a wish is immediately to have
in the temperate air that is always echoing sweet music.

SILVIUS:
It sounds to me like the sacred dwelling of all the gods.
Are they the ones who rule there? And who are your companions?
What are the customs there? What can you tell me of these?

OLYMPIA:
On the mountain's grassy summit, Archesilas sits
and keeps the flocks. He also regulates the heavens,
which I cannot describe because it is so far beyond
the understanding of any human. Full of life
he is yet serene, and in his lap a white lamb nestles
from which comes the food for all who dwell in the sacred wood.
The lamb is the source of health and life for the reborn.
From both of them a light radiates to console
the mournful, cleanse the mind, aid the perplexed, and restore
strength to those who falter. It pours into our souls
a love beyond all measure or any understanding.

You will have already concluded that Archesilas is God,
but may be happy to know that the word in Greek means "ruler."

On either side of their throne is a band of aged satyrs
on top of whose white hair is a crown of woven roses.
They kneel and with their lyres sing praises of the lamb.
After them is a rank of venerable men
dressed in crimson robes and wearing laurel wreaths.
In life they sang at the crossroads hymns to the true god
whom they adored with the terrible pains their bodies endured.
After these is another chorus in robes of white
and wearing garlands of lilies. To this group, we, your children,
are proud to belong. Behind us, garbed in yellow, are more
who sing the praises of god and do their utmost to serve him.
I saw Asylas there when I was led from the forest
up to the mountain peak. The look on his face was serene.

SILVIUS:
I am happy to hear that our Asylus has ascended.
He was a bright example of the ancient faith. He was
a gentle soul. God grant that I may see him again.
But when you passed him did he recognize who you were?

Asylus is Boccaccio's father—who took him in
even though the poet was a bastard. They had quarreled,
the father disapproving of a literary life
(but fathers of legitimate children often say
similar things). Asylus here appears to welcome
Boccaccio's own illegitimate children with great warmth.

OLYMPIA:
He knew me at once and threw his arms about my neck,
kissed me, embraced me, and gave me the warmest possible welcome:
"Silvius' dear child! You have come to join us here.
Let us sing 'Come with me from Lebanon, my bride'
and such sweet hymns." And he led me and bade me kneel down before
the lovely virgin who took me into her arms and made me

one of her handmaidens. "My daughter," she said, "here
you shall join us in our holy chorus and join your spouse
in everlasting marriage. Here you shall be known
no more as Violante, as you were on earth, but now
as Olympia." Then she gave me the raiment that you see.
The entire forest sang in harmonies of unearthly
beauty. Every cave upon the mountain echoed
and there was a sudden glow as from a heatless fire
while petals of various colors drifted down through the air.

*It's all clear enough, I think, except for Asylas' welcome,
which is from the* Song of Songs *and uses the same words
as those in* Purgatory *that greet Beatrice's arrival.*

SILVIUS:
Tell me more. Who is this beautiful virgin queen?

OLYMPIA:
She is the mother of Jove and the daughter of her own son.
She is the gem of heaven, the star of the upper air,
and the surest hope of safety for shepherds everywhere.
She protects their flocks and promises rest from all their labors.
The fauns and nymphs adore her, and Apollo with his lyre
exalts her with the highest praises that he can frame,
proclaiming her his lady. She sits on the father's throne
beside her son's right hand and shines with such effulgent
splendor that the entire forest is much enhanced,
the mountain, the hills, the poles, all brighter from her fair face.
Above her head are flights of swans saluting the mother
who also is bride and daughter of the one eternal light.

SILVIUS:
And while the swans are singing, what do you do, my children?

OLYMPIA:

We gather flowers to braid into our uncut hair
or wander through the forests along its winding streams.
We play in the grass and frolic, singing our praise of the virgin
and her fair son. I cannot think how to describe
the joys of our forest lives, as we cannot say how birds
stretch out their wings and rise into the air to soar
and swoop in graceful circles—as we should love to do.

SILVIUS:

I have often wished for wings. But who will serve as my
Daedalus and teach me how to fly in the sky?
Who will give me wings, tie them on with laces,
and tell me what to do in order to achieve this?

OLYMPIA:

What you must do is feed your hungry brother, offer
cups of milk to the weary stranger, visit the sick,
inquire among the condemned in prison what they might need,
clothe the naked, and, when you can, raise up the fallen.
These little tasks will earn you the feathered wings of eagles
and you will soar to the heights with god directing your journey.

SILVIUS:

You are going now? You leave a mournful father behind.
Can you not stay a moment longer? But, no, she is gone
into the upper air. The pervasive perfume is also
gone with her, and there's nothing left for my senses to clutch.
A moment of hope, yes, but now there will be years
of loss, of tears, and of dwindling old age. Men, wake up!
The morning star is risen. The cows must be driven out
into the pastures to graze where the shadows are fleeing the sun.

XV ℘ Phylostropos

PHYLOSTROPOS:

We've wasted far too much time on these silly nymphs and satyrs.
Look up, Typhlus, and see how the winter constellations
are climbing higher. The trees are leafless now and snow
crowns the mountain peaks. The bitter season approaches
and we must prepare, for the lives of our sheep are much imperiled.

TYPHLUS:

Who cares about mountaintops? The fields around us are golden,
and the chirr of careless cicadas rings out all day long.

Not to defer too long these identifications, the first
Boccaccio takes to mean "conversion," and this is the name
he uses for his teacher, Petrarch. "Typhlus" means "blind"
and, given his self-demeaning habits, it is himself.

PHYLOSTROPOS:

Don't let yourself be fooled. What if the birds are singing?
Hyacinthus was just a boy when Apollo's quoit
hit his head and killed him. Cyparissus, too,
was a youth when he killed Apollo's stag, and he would have died
of grief had the god not turned him into a cypress tree.
Adonis and Meleager also come to mind,

but we need no more examples. Time has a way of flying
or swooping down upon us. Hail has wasted the fields
and we must make haste to move on while the season yet allows.

TYPHLUS:
So what if a few careless or unlucky fellows died?
How can I worry about what terrible things the stars
may or may not be warning me of? No pasture is safe,
but the springs are cool, the grass is good, the climate is mild.
What else can I ask for? The oaks drop down their acorns.
The pines and the hazel trees grow densely together. We know
where the caves are and where the wild beasts have their lairs.
What place is better than this? The sun will come in the spring
to melt the ice and snow, and green leaves will sprout again.

PHYLOSTROPOS:
You have been paying too much attention to Crisis' words.
She promises Hesperides' apples and Ticinus' springs
and the shade of the many laurels that line the Peneus' banks.

You know the Hesperides, but Ticinus? Graduate students
would have to look that up. It's a river up in the Alps
in which you can pan for gold and sometimes do pretty well.
The Peneus, a river in Thessaly, has laurels,
or used to, and those signify poetic success.

Meanwhile, Dyone, crafty with sighs and tears will trap you
and bind you in her chains. Think of the fate of Daphnis
or think of Alexis and learn that what I'm saying is true
and weep with bitter regret at not having paid attention.

Dyone is Venus' mother and, sometimes, Venus herself.
What Phylostropos is saying is that wealth and power can get you

into romantic tangles. Daphnis, for instance is Julius
Caesar and, here, Alexis is our old friend King Roberto.

TYPHLUS:

What's all that to me? All we have is the present,
and right now life is pleasing with leisure the gods would envy,
as well as our hopes, which we know may or may not come true.

PHYLOSTROPOS:

Really? I have it wrong, then, that you are up at cock-crow
while the night is still retreating, with your darling Crisis nagging:
"Typhlus, get up! Head out for the pastures." You wake your sheep
and lead them out through the pathless darkness, feeling your way
with your crook as you go. And more often than not it's raining,
beating down on your head and playing games with your footing,
while the northwind bites your chest or nips at your neck and legs,
making of the skins you are wearing a tasteless joke.
Then summer comes with its heat, and you toss through sleepless nights
sweating on your cot until you get up to repeat
the wintertime drill, except that now there are buzzing gnats
bothering you and your beasts. You have to milk the goats
and work with the milk to make cheese, which isn't an easy chore.
And the sheep have to be washed, for their fleeces are muddy and shitty
and full of burrs that you have to work out. And that's when it's good.
It can also happen that these delicate beasts lie down
and are sick, sick unto death. And what can you do then?
Hope? That's not enough, as you know perfectly well.
Then in the evening you ought to be able to rest at home,
but you can't, having to chop enough wood for the cookstove.
Or harvest the crops from your garden. Or hoe the earth and plant.
This is what you claim the Olympian gods envy?
Your demanding Crisis leaves you no time even for sports.
How long has it been since you entered the wrestling arena?
All your obsessive work, and do you suppose she is grateful?

No, indeed, she hardly gives you a passing thought
but is looking out for her lovers and always recruiting new ones.

TYPHLUS:
You're envious, Phylostropos, and, if I may say so, jealous.
You condemn the embraces you cannot enjoy yourself. What other
lovers do you mean? Are you able to name any?

PHYLOSTROPOS:
You don't want to hear, my friend. As many as stars in the sky!
What beech tree, what woodland cave, what grotto or roadside ditch
has she not found fit for a tryst with one of her moonstruck lads?
And then she discards them all and leaves them to wolves and dogs.

TYPHLUS:
That's blunt enough. But give me names if you would, not merely
general accusations that cannot be refuted.
Who has patronized what you call Crisis' brothel?

PHYLOSTROPOS:
I wish for your sake that you had me stumped there, but not at all.
I'll give you several names and tell you their pitiful stories.
First, you remember Crassus, on Pactolus' golden sands.
Her gifts to him were enormous, but how it came out in the end
was the agony he endured, drinking molten gold.
Remember too the fight between the Thymbrian shepherds
and those from Argolian caves when a catastrophic storm
destroyed so much of the forests. Or think how the bearing sow
plucked from Crisis' lap the unfortunate eastern shepherd.

The Thymbrians and the ones from Argolian caves are Trojans
and Greeks, and either the war was primarily fought for loot
(a plausible idea) or else it could be the story
of Polydorus murdered by the King of Thrace—for gold.

The bearing sow is Tomyris, Queen of the Massegetae,
who cut off the head of Cyrus, the Emperor of Persia,
put the head into a bucket of blood, and threw
the rest of the corpse out on a field for the carrion birds.

There was also a mighty robber who had been a Pharsalian lord
and Crisis possessed him but then on one of her whims left him,
and in grief and chagrin he swallowed the deadly jasper juice.

This is Mithradates, defeated at Pharsalia
by Pompey. Betrayed by his own son, he poisoned himself.
Crushed jasper was thought to be a defense against some poisons,
but apparently too much of it can make one feel unwell.

You won't try to tell me that Crisis once found Dametas pleasing,
but when Pan told him he had to go north and into exile,
she granted him not a single tear, and she took away
his flocks and even his clothes. He sickened and died, and his naked
body was cast out into the street for the dogs,
while gentle Cybele welcomed him into her ample lap.
The farmers laughed at that wretched man. But why go on,
except to say that not many months ago she offered
me her obscene embrace? I managed to decline.

The best guess is that this is Zanobi, who left for France
and in Avignon he caught the plague and died. If so,
then Pan would be the pope. Boccaccio disapproved
of Zanobi's choice in pursuing a diplomatic career
when he could have stayed home and devoted himself to verses.
Petrarch had received a similar Vatican offer,
but unlike poor Zanobi decided to turn it down.

TYPHLUS:

How often have I snatched cute bear cubs from their mother
or crawled out to the end of a trembling bough to pluck
a perfect apple for Crisis! How many times have I snared
pigeons and young doves that I thought were for her sake,
but I suppose that she passed them on to another lover.
Now I will turn to fair Dyone who turns out to be
much less cruel than we have generally imagined.

PHYLOSTROPOS:

Not such a good idea. You want to avoid ruin
of body, mind, and soul? Then you'll want to avoid her!

TYPHLUS:

How can you say such things of a goddess who's always charming?
The rewards she has on offer are like nothing else in the world.

PHYLOSTROPOS:

How many leaves do the trees bring forth each spring? The number
of evils and dangers that she has inflicted on us in the woodland
is greater than that by far. Think of the hair of Nisus,
or Pasiphaë and the bull, or Myrrha and her insane
passion for her father! Think of distracted Medea,
or remember the fires of Troy sparked after all by Paris'
passion for Helen. Remember, too, the mighty Mopsus
whom Love blinded and not in a metaphorical way.
Or there's Hercules in drag, for the love of pretty Omphale . . .
But the list goes on and on. The stories are all well known,
but every man supposes that it can't happen to him
and that somehow he'll get lucky and somehow his luck will last.
You're a fool if you let yourself believe in her sighs and tears
or think that her kisses' meaning endures for more than a breath.
Do not be deluded. Banish such thoughts or else

you will find yourself still here when the frigid winter has come
and then it will be too late for any help or hope.

Mostly it's clear enough. But it may be useful to know
that Mopsus stands for Samson. The others are easy to find.

TYPHLUS:
I'm holding a wolf by its ears. Those things of which you warn me
I long to have. But your words fill me with apprehension.
Abandon Crisis? Turn my back on Dyone's kisses?
On the other hand, I dread the snows, the hail, the sleet,
and all the rages of heaven that howl through the turbulent air.
But I try to calm myself. We have lived through the winter before,
have seen the trees shed leaves and the fields turn white with snow.
What trials other men have endured, I can endure as well,
and we have to take what comes. All I can do is live
as well as I can, avoiding recklessness on the one hand
and, on the other, excessive timidity that would keep me
from indulging in simple pleasures. I'll pipe and sing my songs,
take what Crisis gives me, and accept Dyone's gifts.
Let the one gather flowers and the other make me a wreath.

PHYLOSTROPOS:
I foresee terrible things. The easy warmth of summer
will soon abate and the herds will perish in the cold
fields. The evil nymphs will come for you—I mean
Thlipsis and Lipis, Trini and Peni—to drag you down
below to the dismal woods in Avernus' silent kingdom.

Boccaccio is showing off, using the Greek
to make up the names of the nymphs. Thlipsis means affliction;
Lipis is worry; Trini is grief; and Peni is pain.

TYPHLUS:

But you, my friend, are you not missing the essence of life?
I remember how Epy, once famous in these woods,
sang how death comes to all in mind as well as body.

Absolutely! This gets the grand prize for invention.
Epy is Epicurus. Boccaccio takes it from Petrarch,
who used it to mean the corrupt pope's concubine—and of course
all the worldly pleasures in which he was said to indulge.

PHYLOSTROPOS:

Are you out of your mind? Please tell me you do not agree
with Epy's wicked sayings that everyone else condemns.
Think of Ariston's views, or those of Samos' shepherd,
or remember those Roman farm boys who filled the groves with song.

Ariston is Plato (that was his father's name).
The shepherd from Samos? Pythagoras. And the Roman farm boys
are Virgil, Cicero, Seneca, or any of those stern writers.

Think, most of all, of our Savior, whose blood long ago cleansed
the flocks. He will judge and send the innocent upward to heaven
to join the blessed, while the others will go down into hellfire.
I don't want to see you descend into eternal torment.
Come with me and I'll show you new crags and cliffs to climb.

TYPHLUS:

I'm torn. I hear what you say, Phylostropos, but I fear
to abandon what's sure and real for the will-o'-the-wisp you propose.
No matter how much I respect you, I find this hard to believe.

PHYLOSTROPOS:

Dear boy, let us explore this. What do you think is "sure
and real"? What can you name that Time doesn't snatch away?

The woods that the Ram clads, Orion strips naked again.
Whatever comes into being under heaven passes
away under heaven too. What I offer are fountains
that never run dry in the shade of trees that will stand forever.
Sagittarius comes, the harbinger of disease
and death. Flee his plagues and acknowledge what is sure
and real and then select your path that leads to safety.

TYPHLUS:

Does Arethusa maintain these pastures high on the ridgeline?

PHYLOSTROPOS:

No, I'm afraid this grove is much farther away.

TYPHLUS:

Who is in charge there, tell me? A Greek or is he Egyptian?

PHYLOSTROPOS:

In a green wood beneath the left pole of heaven, the great
Theoschyrus presides as the shepherd above. Among
the thickets a stream of water issues from a rock,
and a few sheep he has chosen and gentle calves drink
and crop the tender grasses that sprout around the stones.
The soil that used to be barren, he has made rich and fertile
and the flocks and herds, hungry and thirsty, are all the more grateful.

"Theoschyrus" comes from the Greek, meaning "son of god."
The water from the rock is what Moses' rod produced,
and that in turn prefigures the blood from Jesus' side.

TYPHLUS:

Why do you tell me these things? Do you want to torment me? My hopes
of seeing this man and taking my place in his grove are dim.
I've stolen a calf from him and trampled his laws underfoot,

and my unholy hands have taken what he has gathered
and given it to Dyone's pigs, I'm ashamed to say.
I fear his strength and his anger. And I worry about my goats
and how they will manage to climb to that lofty outcropping of rock.
Hunger will get them, or mange, or else the unbearable cold.
It's better for me to stay where I am and hang on in this forest.

It has been suggested, debated, and mostly rejected
that the stolen calf represents Boccaccio's seduction
of a nun. If it isn't that, it's clearly some sin or other.

PHYLOSTROPOS:
You underestimate him. Or you don't know him well enough.
His powers of forgiveness are great indeed if you pray
for pardon. Think of Glaucus or after him Amintas.

As before, Glaucus is Peter and Amintas is still Paul.

Let me remind you what a few of the ancients have said
and after that we'll see if you have some refutation.
Your flocks, I say, will be fine, ascending to those sweet pastures .
where the grass is rich and the shade, cool and the water, sweet.
There are no freezing winds. It is never cold. And sickness
never intrudes itself to trouble men or beasts.
No malign star pours down its plagues, but a sacred breeze
soothes and delights not only the body but also the soul.
And the girls there, and the nymphs, and goddesses too will make you
forget all about Crisis and Dyone also, renouncing
trivial pleasures that only distract a man and confuse him.
All you have to do to earn it is to want it.

TYPHLUS:
I do want it. But how did you learn all these details?
Have you been there yourself? Or else who told you these things?

PHYLOSTROPOS:
All the ancient shepherds, Arcadian, Italian,
and Sicilian, too, who were given the chance to climb the peak
are united in reporting what I have just told you.

TYPHLUS:
You have brought new light to my life. But I am full of fear
and I worry about the pitfalls, the falling rocks, the snares,
the whirlpools, and the treacherous footing. I pray to Pales,
unworthy though I am, to help me in my efforts.
And I beg Theoschyrus for mercy that I have not deserved.
I quake with dread! Where can I hide? Where can I flee?
I want to quit these frozen valleys, I am tired
of these infected flocks. I seek those distant woods—
if only I can find a way to break the chains
with which the savage girls have bound me hand and foot.

PHYLOSTROPOS:
You used to be a man of formidable strength, but now
you are suddenly weak, a woman, unable to help yourself.
Break the chains and give yourself back to yourself.
Foolishness is for children. We look for better things
for ourselves and our flocks and herds. But this will require courage.

TYPHLUS:
The arduousness of the journey is fearsome. The giddy height
is daunting. I am lacking in bravery and strength.
What sane man attempts what he knows he can never accomplish?
I hear your recommendation but I am not up to the task.

PHYLOSTROPOS:
You have not yet tried the strength of the chains that bind you.
Vultures circle your head. Resist! Drive them away!
The journey is hard at first, but effort will overcome that,

and the Savior will lend you strength as you climb higher and higher.
Get moving, man! The sun is sinking into the waves.

TYPHLUS:
I will go. But you lead the way. Farewell,
my laurel tree, and goodbye to my flock of shaggy goats.
We go to pluck the palms from trees on the Syrian shore.

XVI 🔖 The Messenger

APPENNINUS:

Tell me, Angelus, who was the shepherd of this amazing
flock of yours? Apollo in Amphisus' verdant valleys
below Oeta watched over such sheep for a time.
Take good care lest wicked or envious men cast
spells upon them. You never can be too careful, you know.

ANGELUS:

Appenninus, your bull is pawing the ground in the meadow
beneath Lyceus' shady dell. Your cows are pregnant.
And I wish them well, and you. You deserve every good fortune.
Don't look down, however, on those who are poor and afflicted:
it's the rich whom fortune envies. And whirlwinds always choose
the tallest trees in the forest upon which to wreak their havoc.

Appenninus, Boccaccio tells us, is his friend
Donato degli Albanzani—who was born and raised
of course in the Apennines. He became godfather
to Petrarch's grandson. The other, Angelus, represents
the other fifteen eclogues, personified and speaking.

APPENNINUS:

I've done well, I admit. Better than I had expected.
But what pasture do you seek with your modest flock?
I count fifteen ewes that you lead through the countryside.
You could pause perhaps and spend some time with me? You see
succulent bushes, springs, comfortable caves, ivy
with bright red berries. What more could anybody want?

ANGELUS:

I'm obliged to you. I will come and mix my herd with yours.
Or, better yet, I'll give them all to you, outright.
There is no greater gift that poor Cerretius could send.
Did you know the old Etruscan when he was in these mountains?

Cerretius is a name Boccaccio gives himself
from his hometown of Certaldo. He is also the old
Etruscan. The fifteen ewes are of course the other poems.

APPENNINUS:

Yes. indeed. I remember seeing the old man
refreshing himself after his strenuous labors. He'd come
and sit with us sometimes in our caves not far from Ravenna.
Or he'd walk in the marshes, woods, and hills of the Veneto.

If it matters, Donato taught for a couple of years in Ravenna
where Boccaccio visited him, and then he moved to Venice.

But look at this poor herd! They're nothing but skin and bones.
He should have sent them on to Silvanus for his care.
He understands diseases and knows how best to cure them.
There is not a shepherd I know or even have ever heard of
to whom Pales has given so much knowledge and power.
The fauns arise to cheer him and the nymphs applaud in their caves
and favorite haunts. The houses of gods are open to him

and the silent dens of Dis. To him this sickly herd
might well be dispatched with hopes for their improvement.

Silvanus is Petrarch, who would, as Boccaccio is saying,
be able to edit the poems and correct some of their defects.

ANGELUS:
He didn't quite have the nerve or confidence to dispatch
so negligible a gift to so wise and mighty a shepherd.
Silvanus is in the habit of caring for herds of kings
and enormous flocks. There's no one Cerretius more reveres.
Whether he plays his pipes or sings, Silvanus' name
is always in his thoughts and often in his mouth,
his lord, patron, example, hope, and acknowledged master.
Second only to him, it's you whom he admires
and to whom he will ever be grateful for your kindness and your
    friendship.
Do not scorn the gift, Appenninus, but rather take it
as a poor expression of love. They're thin, I have to admit,
and they do not give much milk, but their meat, I think, is tasty.
They're better, I venture to say, than Menalcas' beans and apples.
Do him yet another kindness and take his gift.

Menalcas is almost surely Zanobi da Strata, of whom
Boccaccio seems to think often, although not much.

APPENNINUS:
Tell me if you can why they're so skinny. Maybe
there could be some way to put a little meat on their bones.

ANGELUS:
The pastures down at Mount Cerritus are not very good.
No grass, no succulent willow branches, nor any hibiscus.
The goats have to lick the moss-covered rocks and, near the shore,

grab as much as they can of the wild thyme that they find
sprouting among the sea shells. Look at their ragged coats
and their sorry color and see how poorly they have managed.
Fatten them up, if you would. Do what you can, and Silvanus
may also offer suggestions of curative herbs and elixirs.

APPENNINUS:

I've often told Cerretius that those old pastures are wasteland
and there's no point in scratching a crop from that tired dirt.
What keeps him there? Is it cruel Dyone who has him bewitched?
He's old enough to know better. When he was a younger man
Galathea made him a butt of jokes, but now
that he's older and weaker, you'd think he'd have learned that simple
    lesson.

ANGELUS:

No, that's not it. I am sure that he now regrets the time
he wasted on Lycoris and her companions. He's stuck
taking care of his father's meager holdings. He has
no flock, or if he has one, then he is without a pasture.
It's a hard-luck story, boring, banal, but, alas, true.

APPENNINUS:

It's not quite what you think. I know how often Silvanus
has called out to Cerretius offering him fine flocks
and quiet retreats in his Ligurian pastureland.
What more could a man ask for? Great Sicilian leaders,
and Cyprians, too, have come, great knights and satyrs and fauns,
and even gods and goddesses to listen to him sing,
and Pan, struck dumb has laid aside his oaten pipe.
But does our pauper take advantage of such offers?
He appreciates the love and respect that prompt them, but still
he stays put. Let him leave that difficult terrain
and give up on this nonsense of working his father's farm.

The Sicilian is King Roberto; the Cyprian to whom he refers
is Pietro de Lusignano, who was, if you really care,
the son of Ugo IV. They both were kings of Cyprus.

ANGELUS:
Those devoted to pleasure can never understand
how others may chose a different path that leads elsewhere.
An exiguous life he has with his fat cattle consumed,
but Apollo has given him inner riches and he is content.
You see him scratching the dirt and eking out an existence,
but this is what he has chosen. He refused a lucrative offer
to scratch with quills on parchment, helping Egon sing
of his amours. Cerretius declined, having better ways
to spend his time and talent. It wasn't so long ago
that he and I sat talking in the shade of Ceres' oak
to escape the midday heat and I put it to him bluntly:
"Why don't you go to visit your friend Silvanus? He
has invited you often, and you would have an easier time
there than here where you dig in this most unpromising soil."
He stared at the ground and then at a dried-out patch of ivy.
He was silent for quite a time. Than he looked up and said,
"A man who offers everything, really offers nothing.
Egon told me that. And in my younger years,
Midas made me the same kind of open invitation.

Midas here is probably Niccola Acciaiuoli,
but Boccaccio had invitations from Niccolò Orsini,
Hugo di Sanseverino, and King James of Majorca,
all of which he declined—and was proud of having done so.

I have to confess, I accepted Midas' offer. I went
and on my way passed through Baia and saw its spring.
I assumed that preparations were being made—a field,

not big enough for bulls but good for a modest flock
of sheep or goats. When I got there, Stilbon took me in,
and I waited in his house but never had word from Midas.
No field. Not even an invitation to come to dinner.
I was astonished and also angry. What had I done?
I hadn't just shown up. He'd asked me, for heaven's sake!
And I hadn't misbehaved, letting my pigs run wild
to destroy crops in the field, or letting my goats munch
the tender sprouts of vines. Had the whole thing been a joke?
To hell with him, I said, and I came back to this poor
family patch of ground where, knowing what to expect,
I can't be disappointed. And I think I learned my lesson.

Oh, Stilbon! Sorry. Mainardo de' Cavalcanti.

What's the point of wishing? We're anxious, hopeful, fearful . . .
And even when wishes are granted, we find that our lives are no different.
Let us suppose, for argument's sake, that I accept
Silvanus' offer. What if he turns out to be like Midas?
I'd hate to lose such a friend and in such a painful way.
I'd rather lie down and die. It's risky to tempt the gods
who toy with us when they can. Pan has given me gifts
I ought not to spurn. I've learned to be content with little:
I have berries to eat, streams to drink from, shady oaks
beneath which I can sit like this, and lots of leaves
on which to lie down at night. There are some things I lack,
but even a tattered cloak can keep you warm. What's more,
I'm free, I go where I please and do and say what I like.
It's taken me years to realize that these are no small things."
What could I say in reply? He'd spoken the gods' truth.
And therefore I ask you again to accept his modest gift.

APPENNINUS:
You're right. And more important, he is right. I agree
and accept his present. Look at that ewe. She seems to be limping.
Lame? Or maybe pregnant. Perhaps there will be a lamb.
The gift could turn out to be worth more than I supposed.
Look up. We can already see the first stars of the evening.
Have dinner with me. And, Solon, join this flock with ours.